Mrinal K. Das
12 August 1993

AN ATLAS OF INVERTEBRATE STRUCTURE

by W. H. Freeman and Brian Bracegirdle
An Atlas of Invertebrate Structure
An Atlas of Embryology
An Atlas of Histology
An Advanced Atlas of Histology

by Brian Bracegirdle and Patricia H. Miles
An Atlas of Plant Structure: Volume 1
An Atlas of Plant Structure: Volume 2
An Atlas of Chordate Structure

AN ATLAS OF
Invertebrate Structure

W H Freeman *BSc FIBiol*
latterly Head of Biology Department
Chislehurst and Sidcup Grammar School
latterly Chief Examiner 'A'-level Zoology, University of London

Brian Bracegirdle *BSc PhD FIBiol FRPS*

Heinemann Educational Books
London

Heinemann Educational Books Ltd
22 Bedford Square, London WCIB 3HH

London   Edinburgh   Melbourne   Auckland
Singapore   Kuala Lumpur   New Delhi
Ibadan   Nairobi   Johannesburg
Portsmouth (NH)   Kingston

ISBN 0 435 60315 9

First published 1971
Reprinted 1973, 1976, 1977, 1979, 1982, 1985, 1987

Printed and bound in Hong Kong by
Wing King Tong Co. Ltd.

Preface

This book is designed to be used in the laboratory, to help the student interpret his own material. The contents have been chosen to be useful at 'A'-level and in introductory degree courses. We have followed the plan of our earlier atlases of embryology and of histology, and faced a photograph with an interpretive line drawing. All the photographs with the exception of those grouped under no. 166 have been specially made for the book. The pictures included in 166 have been made from transparencies very kindly supplied by Harris Biological Supplies Ltd, and available from them as slides for projection. The drawings have been very fully labelled, for our experience as teachers and as examiners has made it clear that students tend not to label as fully as desirable.

For several species we have provided gross views, photographs of dissections, and photomicrographs at low and high power of various sections. In this way it is possible to understand the structure of an animal much better than with dissection or slide alone; this is the whole basis of relating structure to the physiology and behaviour of a species.

Our own collections of material provided much that was needed for the book but we are most grateful to a number of people for so very willingly providing suitable material. To Dr D. Custance, Dr F. E. G. Cox, The Examination Laboratories of the University of London, Philip Harris Biological Supplies Ltd, Dr Shirley Hawkins, Miss P. H. Miles, Mr P. Nutkins, The Polytechnic of Central London, Mr P. G. Shute, Mr J. Wells, and Dr H. H. Williams we offer our sincere thanks for their generosity in the provision of material.

Miss Patricia Miles has been a great help to us, and we thank her for doing the dissections pictured in the book, as well as advising us on matters of interpretation. The preparation of the book would have taken much longer had it not been for her willing help at many stages of the work.

In our reader, Dr Anne Terry, we were indeed fortunate. No point, however minor escaped her eagle eye, and the book is immeasurably the better for her criticisms. Any errors which remain are our entire responsibility.

W. H. F.
B. B.

1971

COLOUR TRANSPARENCIES FOR PROJECTION

Every picture in this book is available as a 2×2 colour slide for projection from *Philip Harris Biological Supplies Ltd, Oldmixon, Weston-super-Mare, Avon.*

The original master transparencies were made at the same time as the negatives for the pictures in this book, exclusively for this Company. The authors recommend these slides for their quality and moderate cost as excellent aids to the teaching of invertebrate zoology especially in conjunction with this book.

Contents

ARTHROPODA

MOLLUSCA

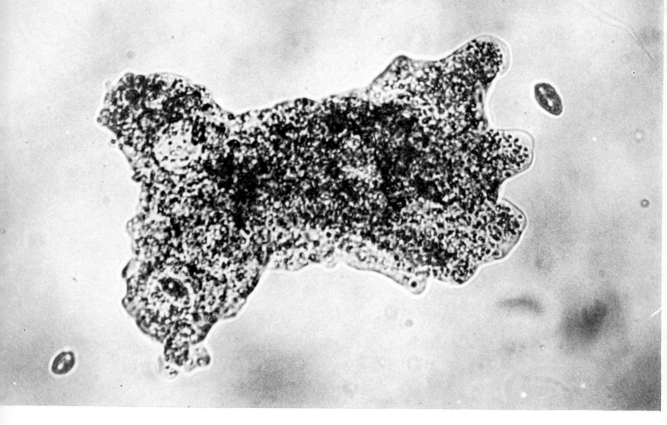

1. *Amoeba*, living, transmitted light. Mag. ×300

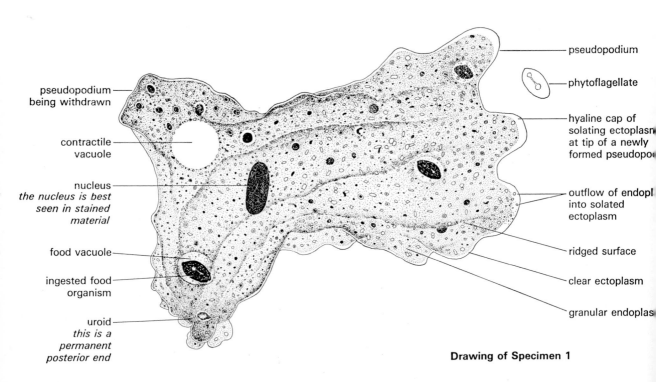

pseudopodium

phytoflagellate

hyaline cap of solating ectoplasm at tip of a newly formed pseudopod

outflow of endopl into solated ectoplasm

ridged surface

clear ectoplasm

granular endoplas

pseudopodium being withdrawn

contractile vacuole

nucleus
the nucleus is best seen in stained material

food vacuole

ingested food organism

uroid
this is a permanent posterior end

Drawing of Specimen 1

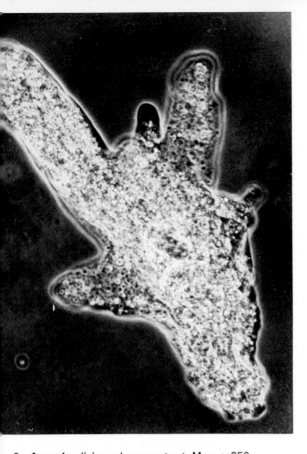

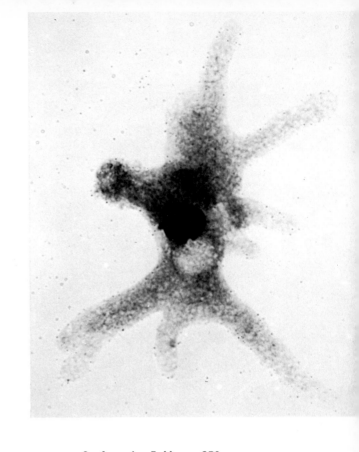

2. **Amoeba**, living, phase contrast. Mag. ×250

3. **Amoeba**, E. Mag. ×250

4. **Foraminifera**, skeletons. Mag. ×35

5. **Radiolaria**, skeletons. Mag. ×40

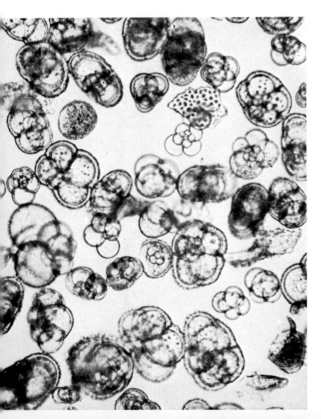

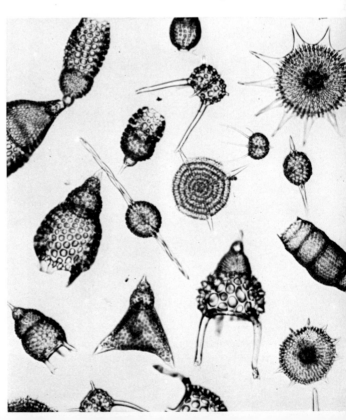

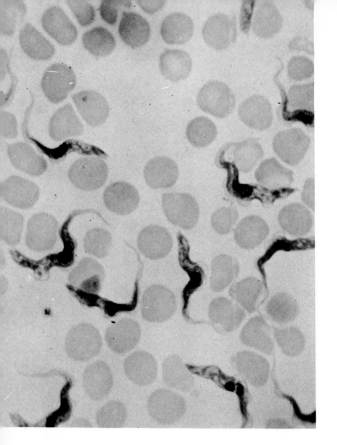

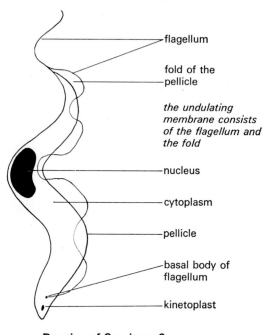

flagellum

fold of the
pellicle

*the undulating
membrane consists
of the flagellum and
the fold*

nucleus

cytoplasm

pellicle

basal body of
flagellum

kinetoplast

Drawing of Specimen 6

6. **Trypanosoma,** in blood film. Mag. ×1100

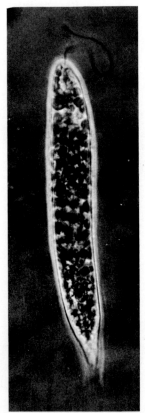

7. **Euglena,** living,
phase contrast.
Mag. ×280

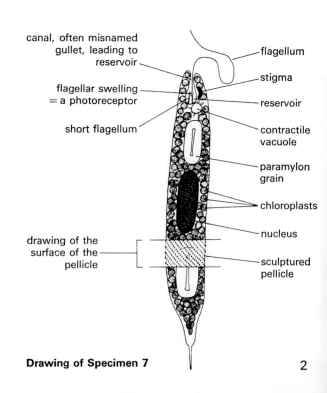

canal, often misnamed
gullet, leading to
reservoir

flagellum

stigma

flagellar swelling
= a photoreceptor

reservoir

short flagellum

contractile
vacuole

paramylon
grain

chloroplasts

nucleus

drawing of the
surface of the
pellicle

sculptured
pellicle

Drawing of Specimen 7

2

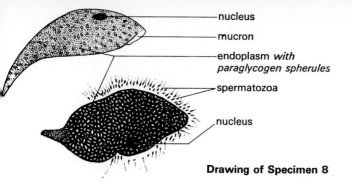

nucleus
mucron
endoplasm *with paraglycogen spherules*
spermatozoa
nucleus

Drawing of Specimen 8

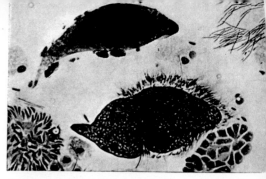

8. *Monocystis*, trophozoites. Mag. ×450

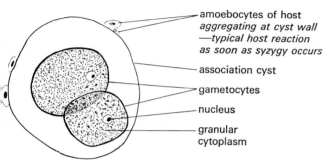

amoebocytes of host *aggregating at cyst wall —typical host reaction as soon as syzygy occurs*
association cyst
gametocytes
nucleus
granular cytoplasm

Drawing of Specimen 9

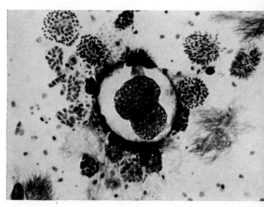

9. *Monocystis*, association cyst. Mag. ×440

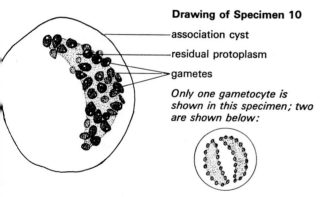

Drawing of Specimen 10

association cyst
residual protoplasm
gametes

Only one gametocyte is shown in this specimen; two are shown below:

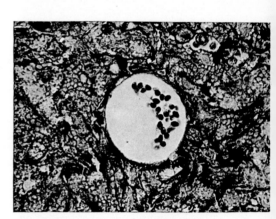

10. *Monocystis*, gametes. Mag. ×575

Drawing of Specimen 11

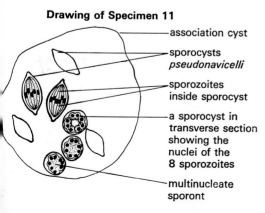

association cyst
sporocysts *pseudonavicelli*
sporozoites inside sporocyst
a sporocyst in transverse section showing the nuclei of the 8 sporozoites
multinucleate sporont

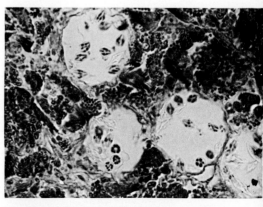

11. *Monocystis*, sporozoites. Mag. ×550

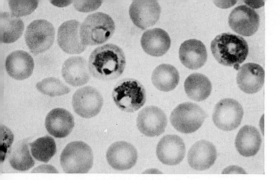

12. **Plasmodium berghei,** trophozoites. Mag. ×1000

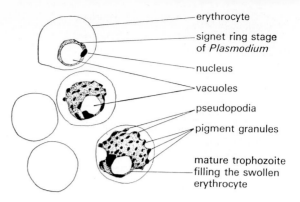

erythrocyte

signet ring stage of *Plasmodium*

nucleus

vacuoles

pseudopodia

pigment granules

mature trophozoite filling the swollen erythrocyte

Drawing of Specimen 12

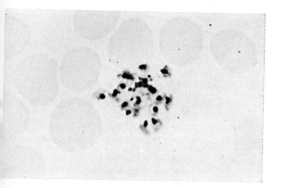

13. **Plasmodium vivax,** merozoites. Mag. ×1400

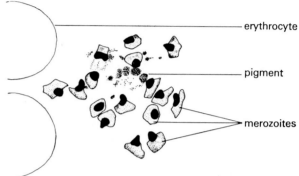

erythrocyte

pigment

merozoites

Drawing of Specimen 13

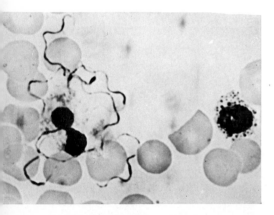

14. **Plasmodium vivax,** microgameto-cytes in blood film. Mag. ×1400

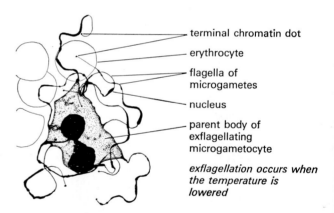

terminal chromatin dot

erythrocyte

flagella of microgametes

nucleus

parent body of exflagellating microgametocyte

exflagellation occurs when the temperature is lowered

Drawing of Specimen 14

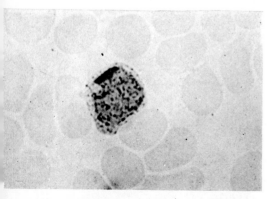

15. **Plasmodium vivax,** macrogameto-cyte in blood film. Mag. ×1400

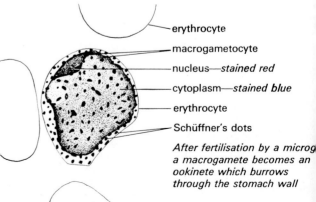

erythrocyte

macrogametocyte

nucleus—*stained red*

cytoplasm—*stained blue*

erythrocyte

Schüffner's dots

After fertilisation by a microg a macrogamete becomes an ookinete which burrows through the stomach wall

Drawing of Specimen 15

4

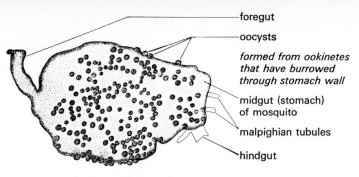

foregut

oocysts

formed from ookinetes that have burrowed through stomach wall

midgut (stomach) of mosquito

malpighian tubules

hindgut

Drawing of Specimen 16

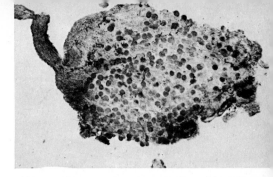

16. *Plasmodium,* oocysts on mosquito midgut, E. Mag. ×35

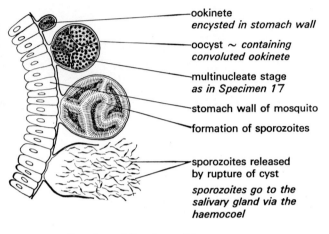

ookinete
encysted in stomach wall

oocyst ~ *containing convoluted ookinete*

multinucleate stage *as in Specimen 17*

stomach wall of mosquito

formation of sporozoites

sporozoites released by rupture of cyst

sporozoites go to the salivary gland via the haemocoel

Drawing of Specimen 17

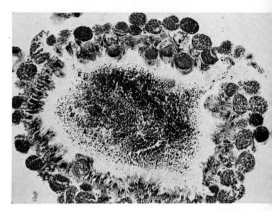

17. *Plasmodium,* oocysts on mosquito midgut, TS. Mag. ×45

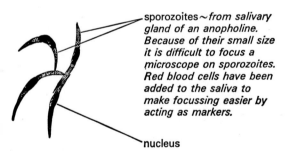

sporozoites ~ *from salivary gland of an anopholine. Because of their small size it is difficult to focus a microscope on sporozoites. Red blood cells have been added to the saliva to make focussing easier by acting as markers.*

nucleus

Drawing of Specimen 18

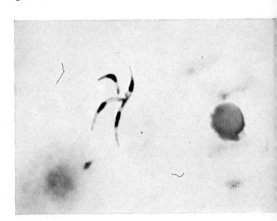

18. *Plasmodium berghei,* sporozoites in mosquito saliva. Mag. ×1400

Drawing of Specimen 19

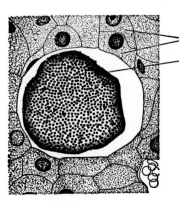

liver cells

schizont
For several days after infection by a mosquito bite malaria parasites are absent from the blood; in mammalian malaria schizogony occurs in the liver during this exo-erythrocytic phase. The merozoites released can infect blood cells and liver cells.

19. *Plasmodium vivax,* pre-erythrocytic stage in TS human liver. Mag. ×600

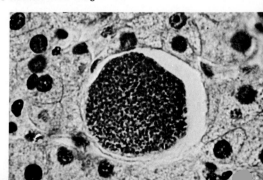

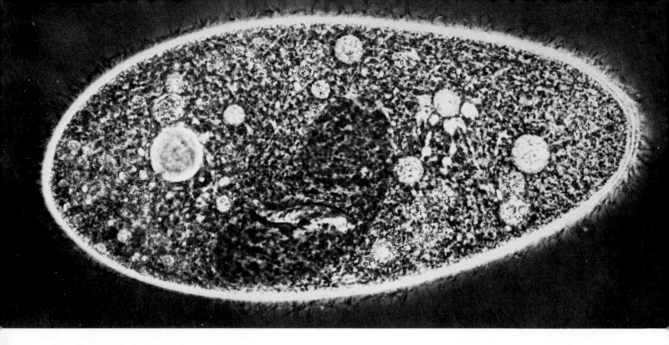

20. *Paramecium*, living, phase contrast. Mag. ×750

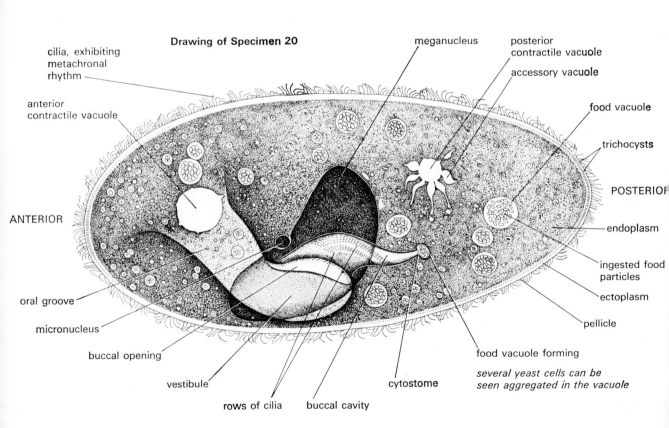

Drawing of Specimen 20

cilia, exhibiting metachronal rhythm

anterior contractile vacuole

meganucleus

posterior contractile vacuole

accessory vacuole

food vacuole

trichocysts

POSTERIOR

ANTERIOR

endoplasm

ingested food particles

ectoplasm

pellicle

oral groove

micronucleus

buccal opening

vestibule

rows of cilia

buccal cavity

cytostome

food vacuole forming

several yeast cells can be seen aggregated in the vacuole

BINARY FISSION *Paramecium reproduces by binary fission and any of the following stages may be seen:*

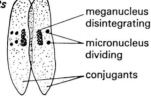

micronucleus dividing mitotically

meganucleus dividing amitotically

cytoplasm constricting as in Specimen 21

two individuals produced by transverse fission

CONJUGATION *The two conjugants meet their oral surfaces to exchange nuclear material. The theoretical picture shown in drawing is rarely achieved, the stage shown in Specimen 22 is more usually seen.*

meganucleus disintegrating

micronucleus dividing

conjugants

pigment lodged in pits

ridges

discharged trichocysts

SCULPTURED PELLICLE
Pigment lodged in the pits shows the sculpturing of the pellicle. Some of the trichocysts lying in the ridges have discharged their threads. The oral groove and buccal opening are clear in this surface view of Specimen 23.

Drawings of Specimens 21, 22, and 23

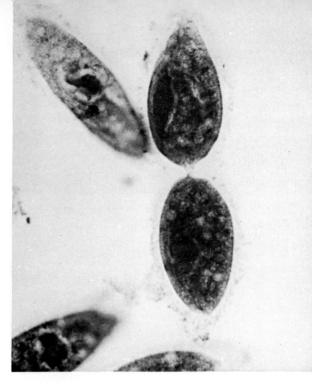

21. **Paramecium**, binary fission. Mag. ×175

23. **Paramecium**, pellicle. Mag. ×135

22. **Paramecium**, conjugation. Mag. ×120

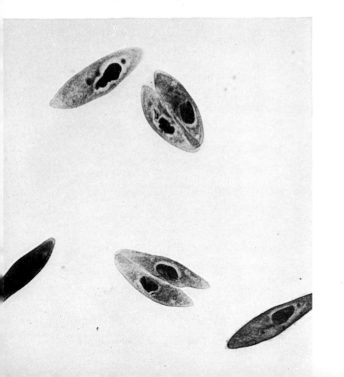

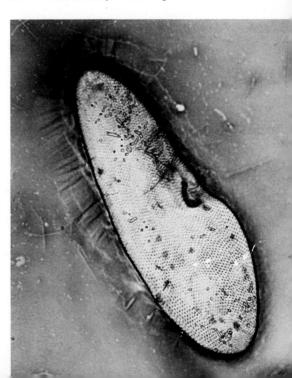

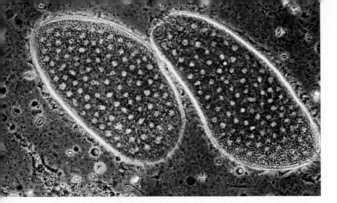

24. **Opalina,** living, phase contrast. Mag. ×350

25. **Balantidium,** E. Mag. ×600

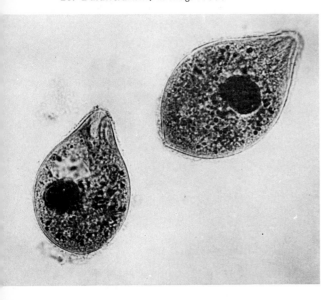

26. **Nyctotherus,** E. Mag. ×950

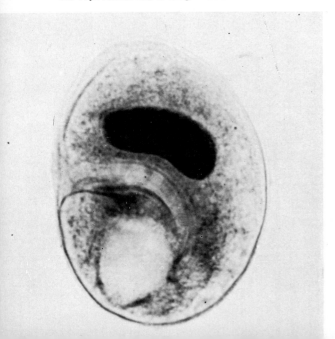

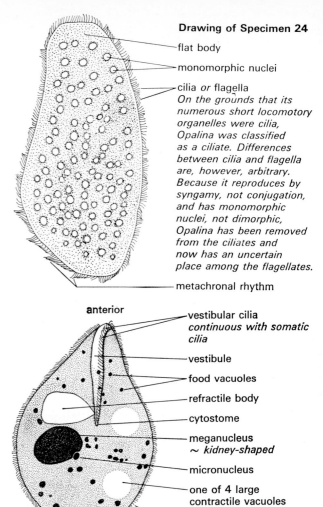

Drawing of Specimen 24

flat body

monomorphic nuclei

cilia *or* flagella
On the grounds that its numerous short locomotory organelles were cilia, Opalina was classified as a ciliate. Differences between cilia and flagella are, however, arbitrary. Because it reproduces by syngamy, not conjugation, and has monomorphic nuclei, not dimorphic, Opalina has been removed from the ciliates and now has an uncertain place among the flagellates.

metachronal rhythm

anterior

vestibular cilia
continuous with somatic cilia

vestibule

food vacuoles

refractile body

cytostome

meganucleus
~ *kidney-shaped*

micronucleus

one of 4 large contractile vacuoles
—*there are many small or*

cilia
arranged in longitudinal lines

posterior

Drawing of Specimen 25

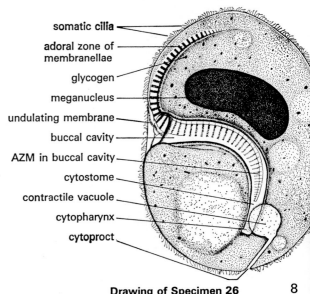

somatic cilia

adoral zone of membranellae

glycogen

meganucleus

undulating membrane

buccal cavity

AZM in buccal cavity

cytostome

contractile vacuole

cytopharynx

cytoproct

Drawing of Specimen 26

8

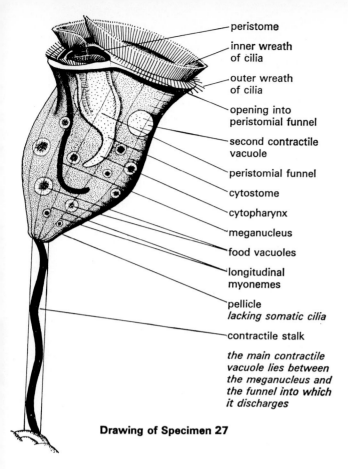

- peristome
- inner wreath of cilia
- outer wreath of cilia
- opening into peristomial funnel
- second contractile vacuole
- peristomial funnel
- cytostome
- cytopharynx
- meganucleus
- food vacuoles
- longitudinal myonemes
- pellicle *lacking somatic cilia*
- contractile stalk

the main contractile vacuole lies between the meganucleus and the funnel into which it discharges

Drawing of Specimen 27

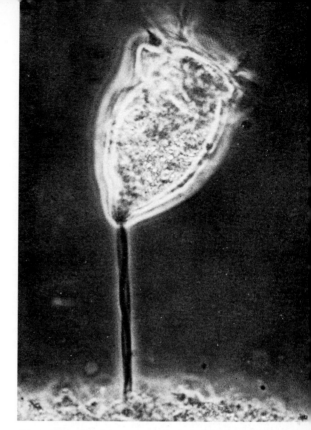

27. **Vorticella**, living, phase contrast. Mag. ×350

28. **Euplotes**, living, phase contrast. Mag. ×250

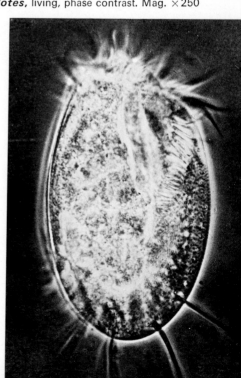

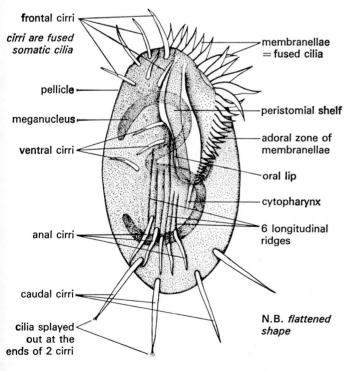

- frontal cirri
- *cirri are fused somatic cilia*
- pellicle
- meganucleus
- ventral cirri
- anal cirri
- caudal cirri
- cilia splayed out at the ends of 2 cirri
- membranellae = fused cilia
- peristomial **shelf**
- adoral zone of membranellae
- oral **lip**
- cytopharynx
- 6 longitudinal ridges

N.B. *flattened shape*

Drawing of Specimen 28

9

29. **Leucosolenia**, E, showing spicules. Mag. ×50

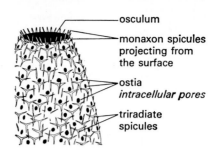

osculum
monaxon spicules
projecting from
the surface
ostia
intracellular pores
triradiate
spicules

Drawing of Specimen 29

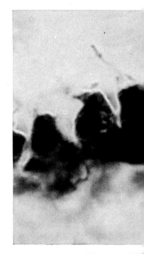

30. **Choanocytes in TS *Grantia*,** phase contrast. Mag. ×85(

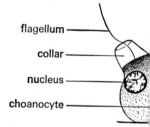

flagellum
collar
nucleus
choanocyte

Drawing of Specimen 30

31. **Gemmules of freshwater sponge,** E. Mag. ×550

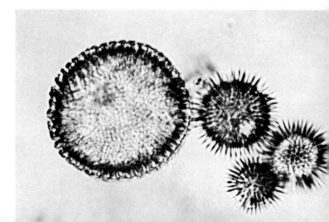

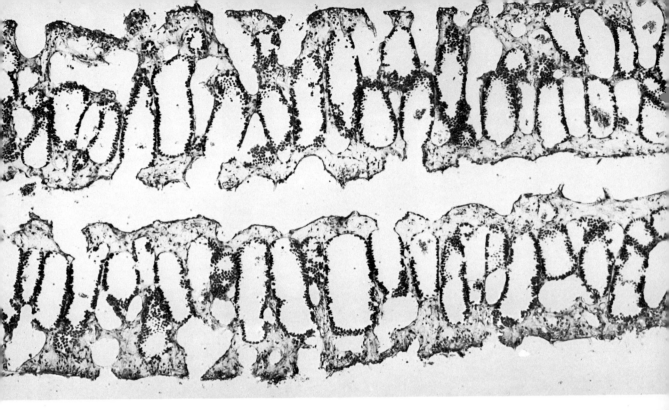

32. *Grantia*, TS. Mag. ×120

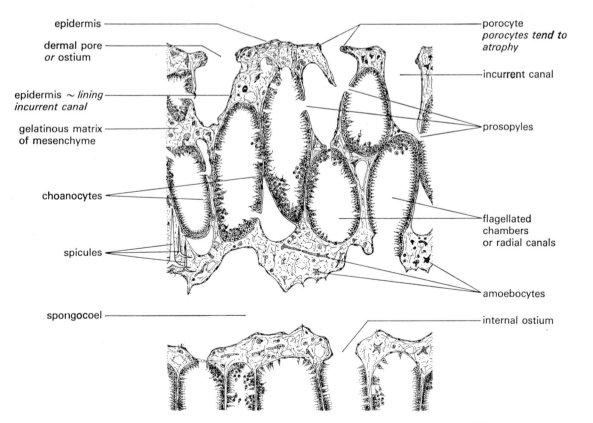

epidermis ————————

dermal pore
or ostium ————————

epidermis ~ *lining
incurrent canal* ————————

gelatinous matrix
of mesenchyme ————————

choanocytes ————————

spicules ————————

spongocoel ————————

porocyte
*porocytes tend to
atrophy*

————————— incurrent canal

————————— prosopyles

————————— flagellated
chambers
or radial canals

————————— amoebocytes

————————— internal ostium

Drawing of Specimen 32

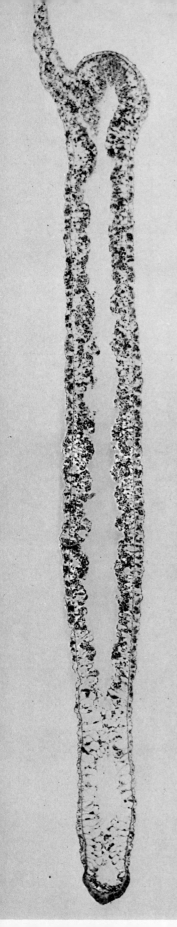

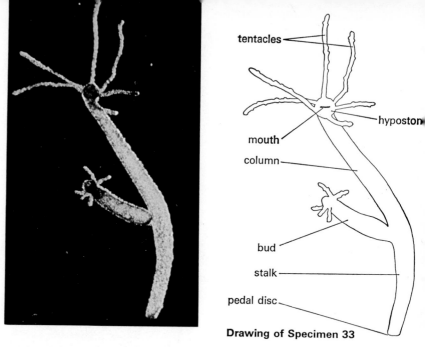

tentacles

hypostome

mouth

column

bud

stalk

pedal disc

Drawing of Specimen 33

33. *Hydra*, E, with bud, living. Mag. ×145

Drawing of Specimen 34

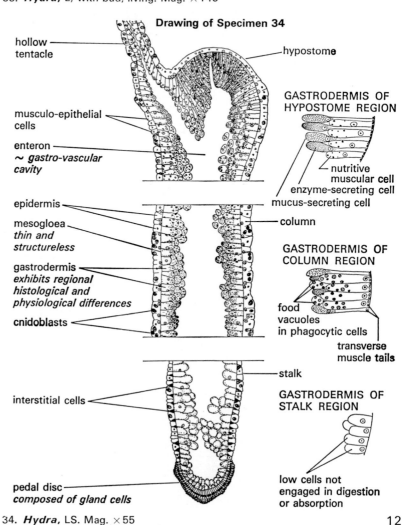

hollow tentacle

hypostome

musculo-epithelial cells

enteron
~ *gastro-vascular cavity*

GASTRODERMIS OF HYPOSTOME REGION

nutritive muscular **cell**
enzyme-secreting **cell**
mucus-secreting cell

epidermis

mesogloea
thin and structureless

column

gastrodermis
exhibits regional histological and physiological differences

cnidoblasts

GASTRODERMIS OF COLUMN REGION

food vacuoles in phagocytic cells

transverse muscle **tails**

stalk

interstitial cells

GASTRODERMIS OF STALK REGION

pedal disc
composed of gland cells

low cells not engaged in digestion or absorption

34. *Hydra*, LS. Mag. ×55

12

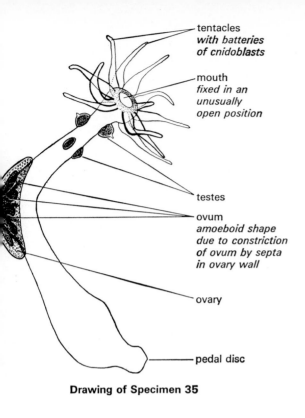

tentacles
*with batteries
of cnidoblasts*

mouth
*fixed in an
unusually
open position*

testes

ovum
*amoeboid shape
due to constriction
of ovum by septa
in ovary wall*

ovary

pedal disc

Drawing of Specimen 35

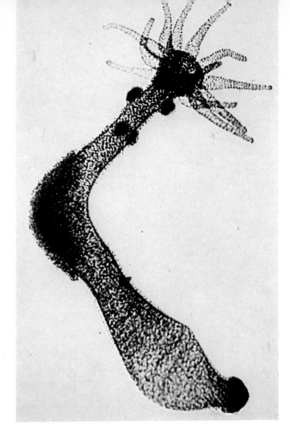

35. **Hydra**, E, with testes and ovary. Mag. ×100

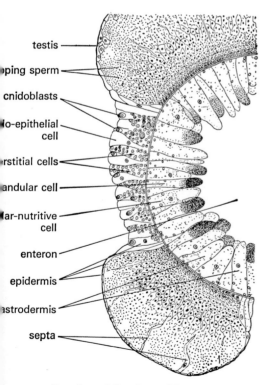

testis

ping sperm

cnidoblasts

o-epithelial
cell

rstitial cells

andular cell

ar-nutritive
cell

enteron

epidermis

astrodermis

septa

Drawing of Specimen 36

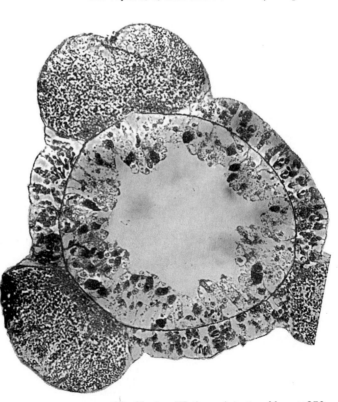

36. **Hydra**, TS through testes. Mag. ×250

13

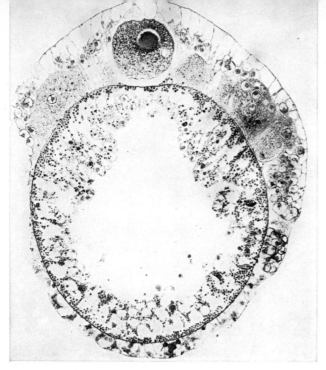

37. *Hydra*, TS through ovary. Mag. ×250

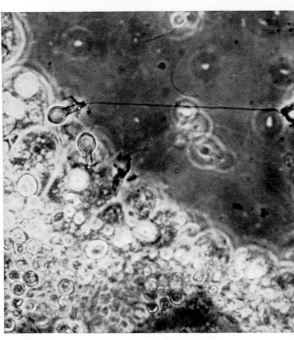

38. *Hydra*, nematoblasts on tentacle, living, phase contrast
Mag. ×800

Drawing of Specimen 37

lobes of the
yolk-laden ovum
*food provided by
disintegrating
interstitial cells*

epidermis

mesogloea

ovary

septum

zoochlorellae
symbiotic algae

gastrodermis
*vacuolated cells,
some of which
are secretory*

enteron

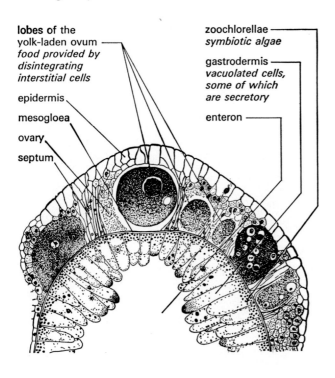

musculo-epithelial cell

barb

discharged tube

cnidocyst

operculum

stenotele type
of cnidocyst

desmonemes and
isorhizas

stenotele = *penetrant*
desmoneme = *volvent*
isorhiza = *glutinant*

cnidocil *or* trigger

supporting rods

operculum *or* lid

barbs

butt

cnidocyst capsule

coiled tube

supporting fibres

cnidoblast cell

nucleus

stenotele type

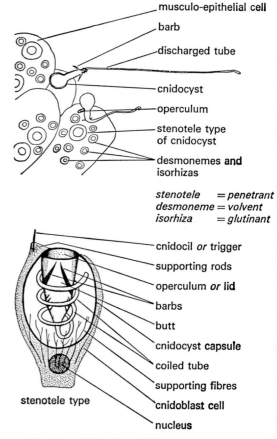

Drawing of Specimen 38

14

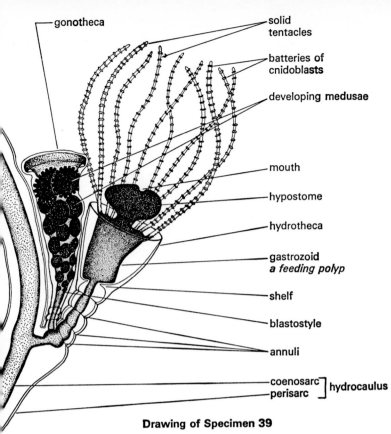

gonotheca

solid
tentacles

batteries of
cnidoblasts

developing **medusae**

mouth

hypostome

hydrotheca

gastrozoid
a feeding polyp

shelf

blastostyle

annuli

coenosarc ⎤ **hydrocaulus**
perisarc ⎦

Drawing of Specimen 39

39. **Obelia**, E, part of colony. Mag. ×30

40. **Obelia**, medusa E. Mag. ×20

Drawing of Specimen 40

solid
tentacles

sub-umbrella
surface

gonad

radial canal

manubrium

oral tentacles

circular canal

statocyst
8, arranged adradially

basal swellings
of tentacles
*aggregations of interstitial cells
developing into cnidoblasts*

15

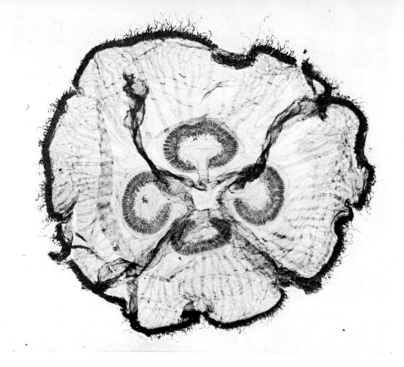

41. *Aurelia,* medusa E. Mag. ×2

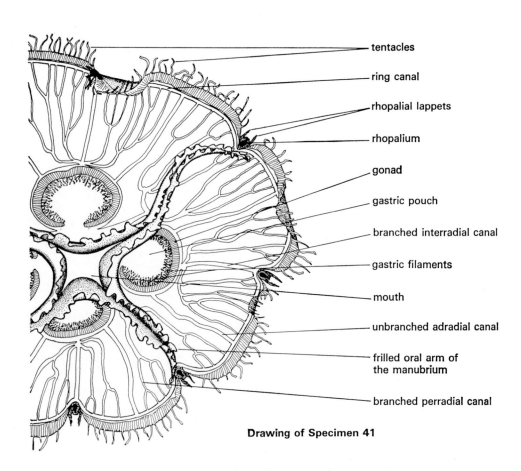

tentacles

ring canal

rhopalial lappets

rhopalium

gonad

gastric pouch

branched interradial canal

gastric filaments

mouth

unbranched adradial canal

frilled oral arm of
the manubrium

branched perradial canal

Drawing of Specimen 41

Drawing of Specimen 42

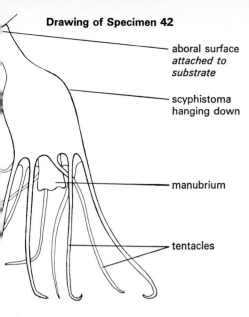

aboral surface *attached to substrate*

scyphistoma hanging down

manubrium

tentacles

42. *Aurelia*, scyphistomae E, living. Mag. ×25

Drawing of Specimen 43

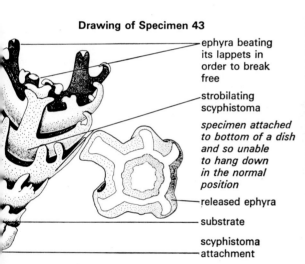

ephyra beating its lappets in order to break free

strobilating scyphistoma

specimen attached to bottom of a dish and so unable to hang down in the normal position

released ephyra

substrate

scyphistoma attachment

43. *Aurelia*, scyphistoma strobilating E, living. Mag. ×50

44. *Aurelia*, ephyra E. Mag. ×30

Drawing of Specimen 44

lappets

rhopalium

oral arm

stomach *gastric filaments not visible*

mouth

manubrium

perradial canal

adradial canal

interradial canal

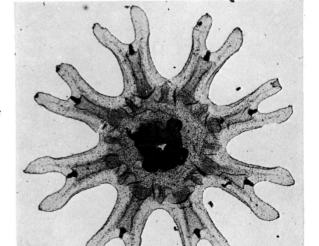

17

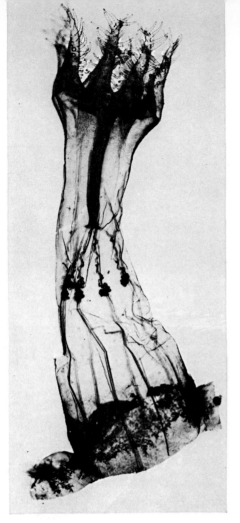

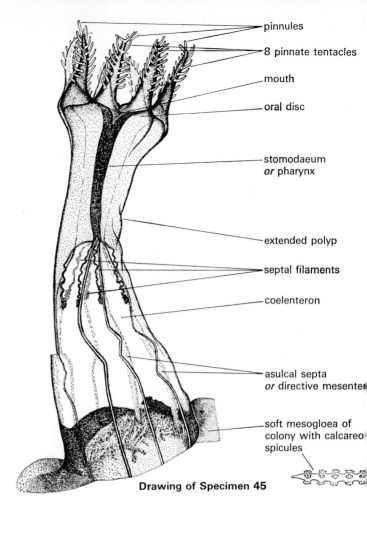

pinnules

8 pinnate tentacles

mouth

oral disc

stomodaeum *or* pharynx

extended polyp

septal filaments

coelenteron

asulcal septa *or* directive mesenter

soft mesogloea of colony with calcareo spicules

Drawing of Specimen 45

45. *Alcyonium*, polyp E. Mag. ×10

46. *Alcyonium*, colony TS. Mag. ×5

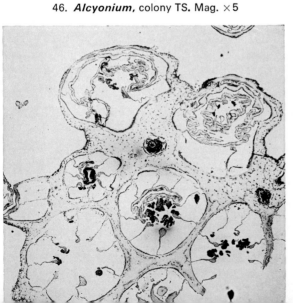

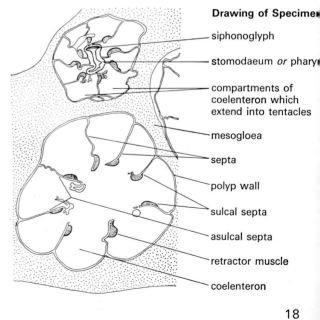

Drawing of Specime

siphonoglyph

stomodaeum *or* phary

compartments of coelenteron which extend into tentacles

mesogloea

septa

polyp wall

sulcal septa

asulcal septa

retractor muscle

coelenteron

18

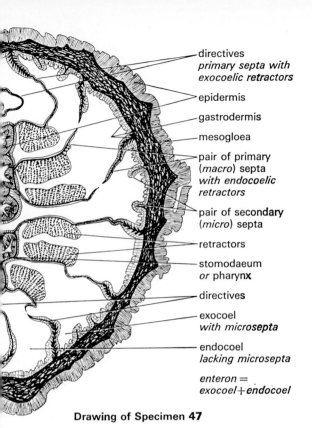

directives
*primary septa with
exocoelic retractors*

epidermis

gastrodermis

mesogloea

pair of primary
(*macro*) septa
*with endocoelic
retractors*

pair of secondary
(*micro*) septa

retractors

stomodaeum
or pharynx

directives

exocoel
with microsepta

endocoel
lacking microsepta

*enteron =
exocoel + endocoel*

Drawing of Specimen 47

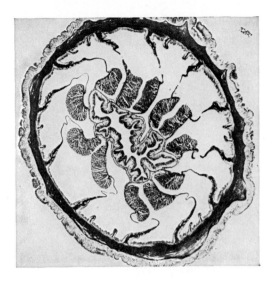

47. *Halcampa,* TS through pharynx. Mag. ×20

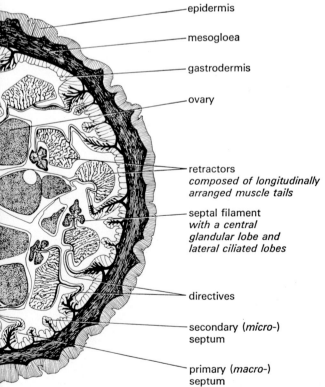

epidermis

mesogloea

gastrodermis

ovary

retractors
*composed of longitudinally
arranged muscle tails*

septal filament
*with a central
glandular lobe and
lateral ciliated lobes*

directives

secondary (*micro-*)
septum

primary (*macro-*)
septum

Drawing of Specimen 48

48. *Halcampa,* TS below pharynx. Mag. ×20

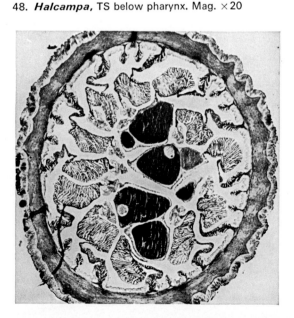

19

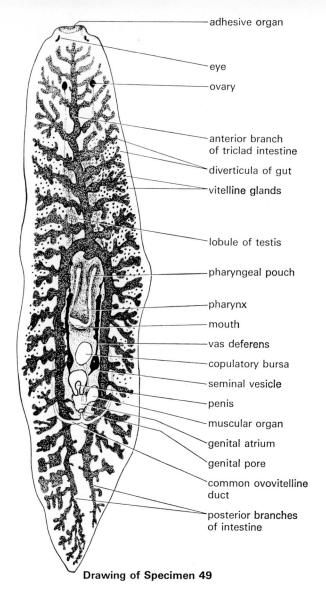

- adhesive organ
- eye
- ovary
- anterior branch of triclad intestine
- diverticula of gut
- vitelline glands
- lobule of testis
- pharyngeal pouch
- pharynx
- mouth
- vas deferens
- copulatory bursa
- seminal vesicle
- penis
- muscular organ
- genital atrium
- genital pore
- common ovovitelline duct
- posterior branches of intestine

Drawing of Specimen 49

49. *Dendrocoelum*, E. Mag. ×15

50. **Planarian**, TS. Mag. ×70

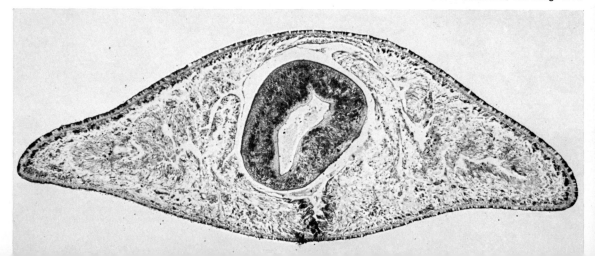

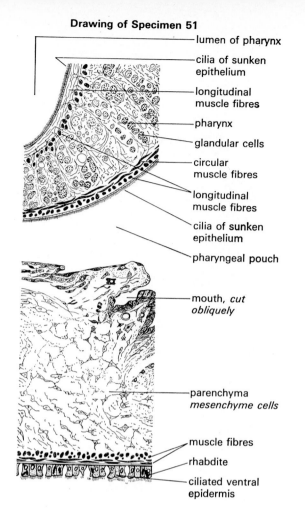

Drawing of Specimen 51

- lumen of pharynx
- cilia of sunken epithelium
- longitudinal muscle fibres
- pharynx
- glandular cells
- circular muscle fibres
- longitudinal muscle fibres
- cilia of sunken epithelium
- pharyngeal pouch

- mouth, *cut obliquely*

- parenchyma *mesenchyme cells*

- muscle fibres
- rhabdite
- ciliated ventral epidermis

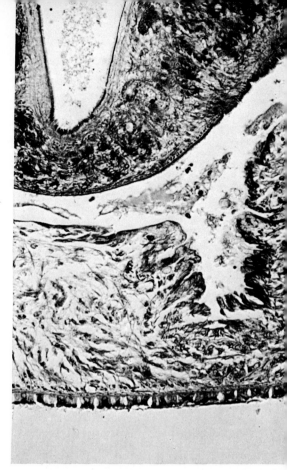

51. Planarian, TS through pharynx. Mag. × 350

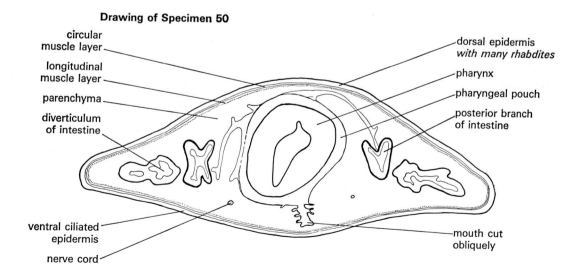

Drawing of Specimen 50

- circular muscle layer
- longitudinal muscle layer
- parenchyma
- diverticulum of intestine

- dorsal epidermis *with many rhabdites*
- pharynx
- pharyngeal pouch
- posterior branch of intestine

- ventral ciliated epidermis
- nerve cord
- mouth cut obliquely

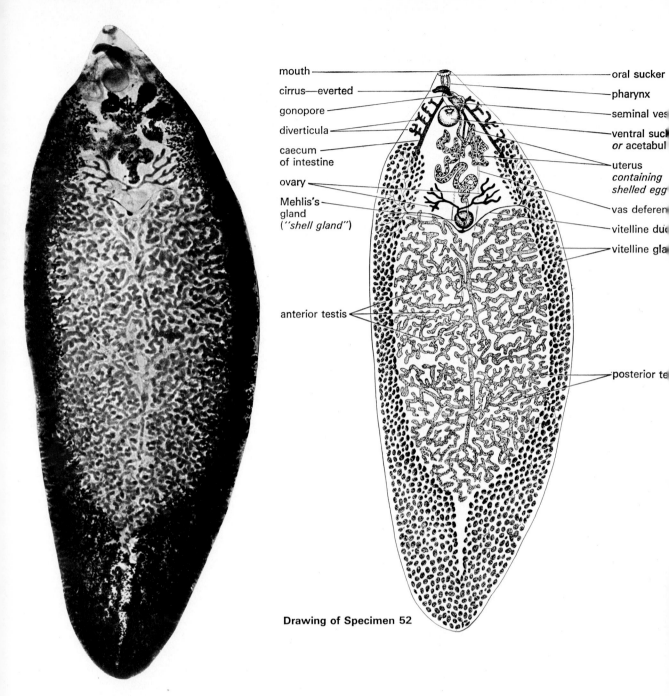

mouth ——————————— oral sucker

cirrus—everted ——————— pharynx

gonopore ————————— seminal ves

diverticula ————— ventral suc
or acetabul

caecum ————— uterus
of intestine containing
shelled egg

ovary ————

Mehlis's ———— vas deferen
gland
("shell gland") vitelline du

vitelline gl

anterior testis ———<

posterior te

Drawing of Specimen 52

52. *Fasciola*, E. Mag. ×7

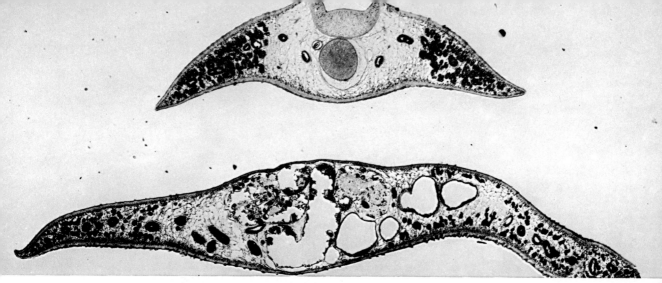

53. *Fasciola,* TS through ventral sucker and through body. Mag. ×25

Drawing of Specimen 53

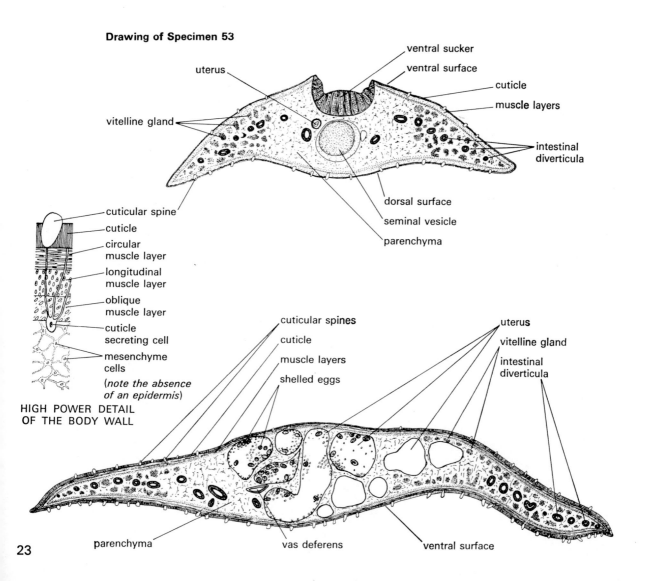

ventral sucker

ventral surface

cuticle

muscle layers

uterus

intestinal diverticula

vitelline gland

dorsal surface

seminal vesicle

parenchyma

cuticular spine

cuticle

circular muscle layer

longitudinal muscle layer

oblique muscle layer

cuticle secreting cell

mesenchyme cells

(*note the absence of an epidermis*)

HIGH POWER DETAIL OF THE BODY WALL

cuticular spines

cuticle

muscle layers

shelled eggs

uterus

vitelline gland

intestinal diverticula

parenchyma

vas deferens

ventral surface

23

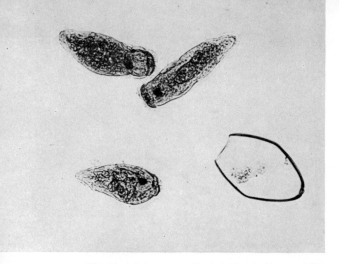

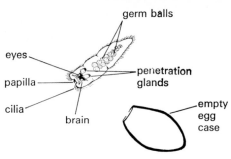

germ balls

eyes

papilla

cilia

penetration
glands

brain

empty
egg
case

Drawing of Specimen 54

54. *Fasciola*, egg and miracidia, E. Mag. × 650

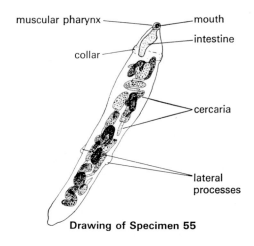

muscular pharynx

mouth

intestine

collar

cercaria

lateral
processes

Drawing of Specimen 55

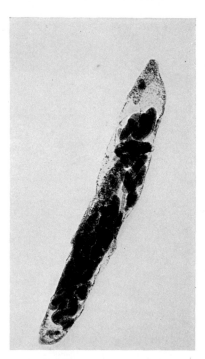

55. *Fasciola*, redia, E. Mag. × 300

56. *Fasciola*, cercariae, E. Mag. × 500

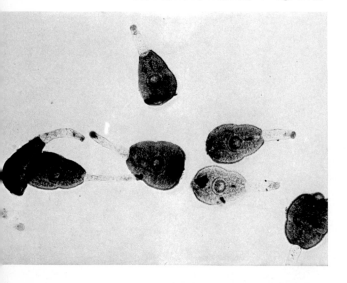

Drawing of Specimen 56

mouth

oral
sucker

bifid
intestine

ventral
sucker

cystogenous
gland

rudiment of
reproductive
organs

tail

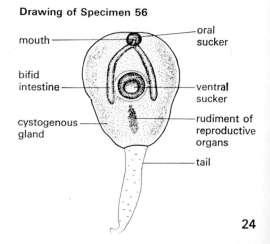

24

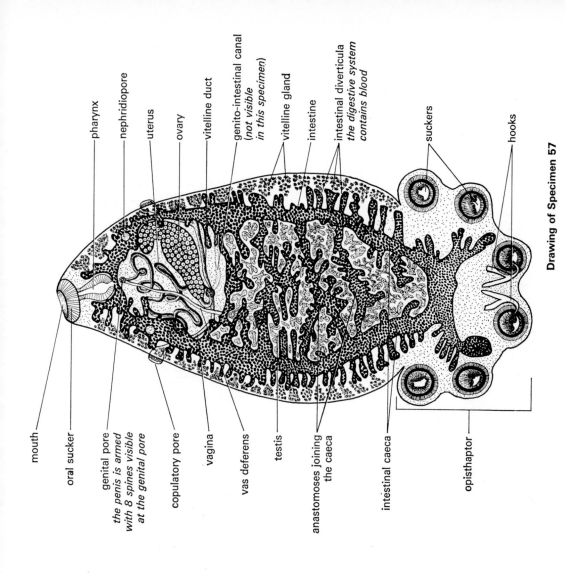

mouth
oral sucker
genital pore
the penis is armed
with 8 spines visible
at the genital pore
copulatory pore
vagina
vas deferens
testis
anastomoses joining
the caeca
intestinal caeca
opisthaptor

pharynx
nephridiopore
uterus
ovary
vitelline duct
genito-intestinal canal
(*not visible*
in this specimen)
vitelline gland
intestine
intestinal diverticula
the digestive system
contains blood
suckers
hooks

Drawing of Specimen 57

57. *Polystoma*, E. Mag. ×25

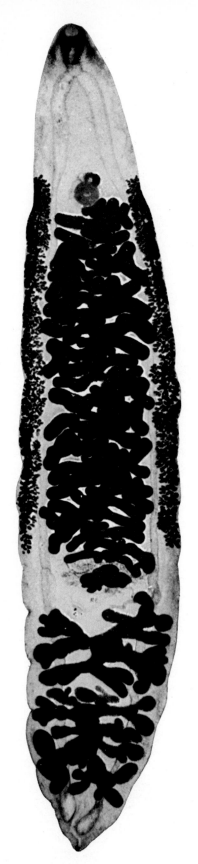

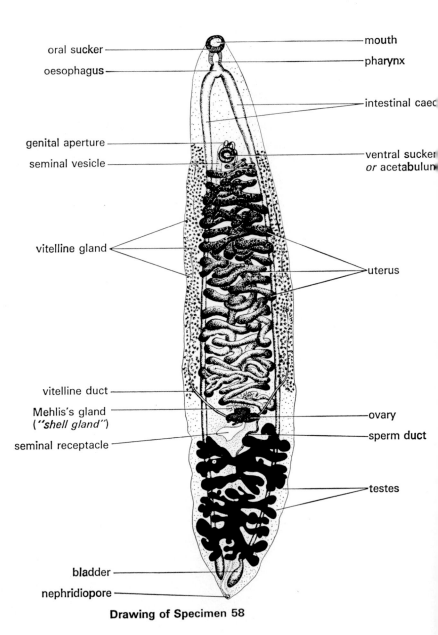

oral sucker — — mouth

— pharynx

oesophagus —

— intestinal caec

genital aperture —

seminal vesicle — — ventral sucker
or acetabulum

vitelline gland —

— uterus

vitelline duct —

Mehlis's gland
(*"shell gland"*) — — ovary

— sperm duct

seminal receptacle —

— testes

bladder —

nephridiopore —

Drawing of Specimen 58

58. *Opisthorchis,* E. Mag. ×20

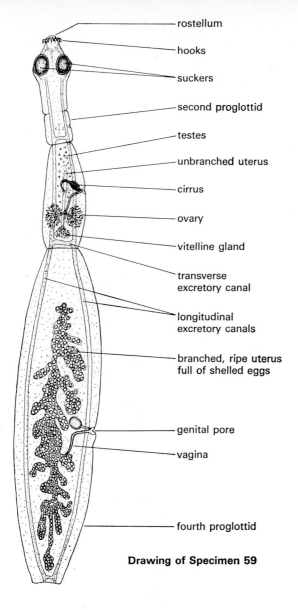

— rostellum

— hooks

— suckers

— second proglottid

— testes

— unbranched uterus

— cirrus

— ovary

— vitelline gland

— transverse excretory canal

— longitudinal excretory canals

— branched, ripe uterus full of shelled eggs

— genital pore

— vagina

— fourth proglottid

Drawing of Specimen 59

59. *Echinococcus*, E. Mag. ×12

60. *Phyllobothrium*, scolex E. Mag. ×18

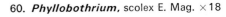

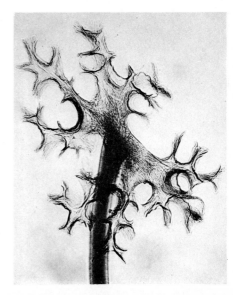

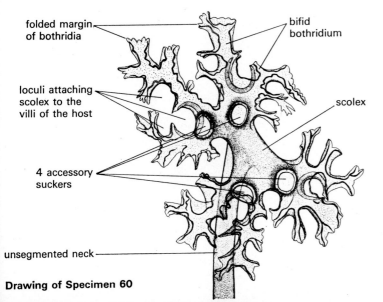

folded margin of bothridia

bifid bothridium

loculi attaching scolex to the villi of the host

scolex

4 accessory suckers

unsegmented neck

Drawing of Specimen 60

61. *Taenia*, scolex E. Mag. ×12

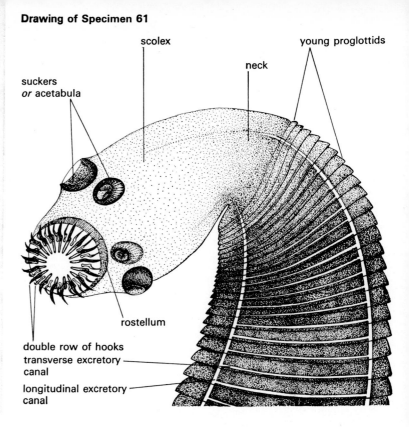

scolex

suckers *or* acetabula

neck

young proglottids

rostellum

double row of hooks

transverse excretory canal

longitudinal excretory canal

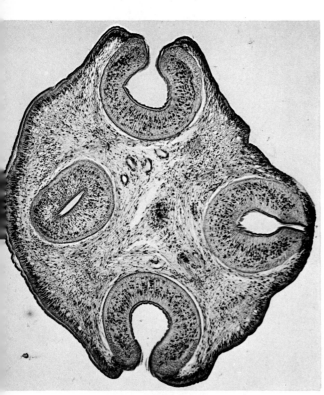

62. *Taenia*, scolex TS. Mag. ×40

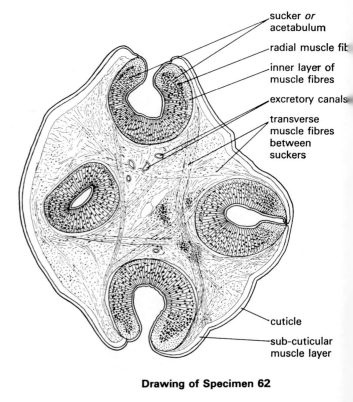

sucker *or* acetabulum

radial muscle fib

inner layer of muscle fibres

excretory canals

transverse muscle fibres between suckers

cuticle

sub-cuticular muscle layer

Drawing of Specimen 62

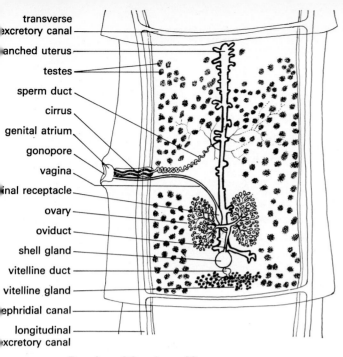

transverse excretory canal
branched uterus
testes
sperm duct
cirrus
genital atrium
gonopore
vagina
seminal receptacle
ovary
oviduct
shell gland
vitelline duct
vitelline gland
nephridial canal
longitudinal excretory canal

Drawing of Specimen 63

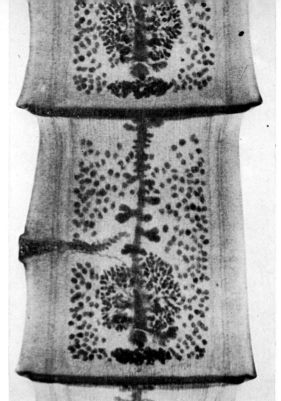

63. *Taenia* mature proglottid E. Mag. ×30

64. *Taenia*, gravid proglottid E. Mag. ×20

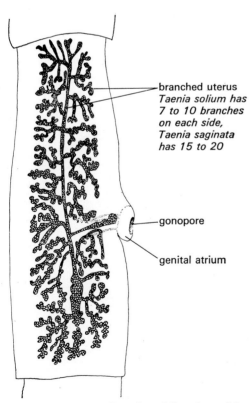

branched uterus
Taenia solium has 7 to 10 branches on each side, Taenia saginata has 15 to 20

gonopore

genital atrium

Drawing of Specimen 64

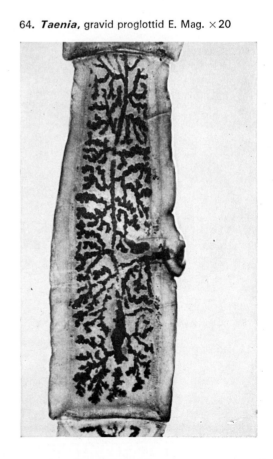

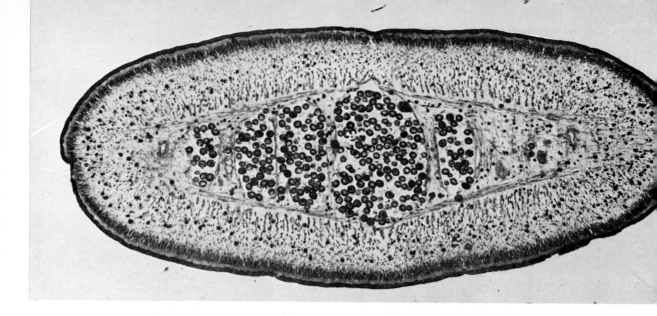

65. *Taenia,* gravid proglottid TS. Mag. ×100

Drawing of Specimen 65

DIAGRAM OF INTEGUMENT
(*based on electron micrographs*)

integument

cortex

medulla

microvilli

integument ~ *living extension of
integument secreting cells*

mitochondria

circular muscle fibres

longitudinal muscle fibres

integument secreting cell

parenchyma

longitudinal muscle fibres

longitudinal
excretory canal

position of lateral
nerve cord

parenchyma

integument secreting cells

muscle layer

testis remnant

transverse muscle

dorso-ventral muscle

egg capsules containing
embryos

branches of uterus

longitudinal muscle fibres

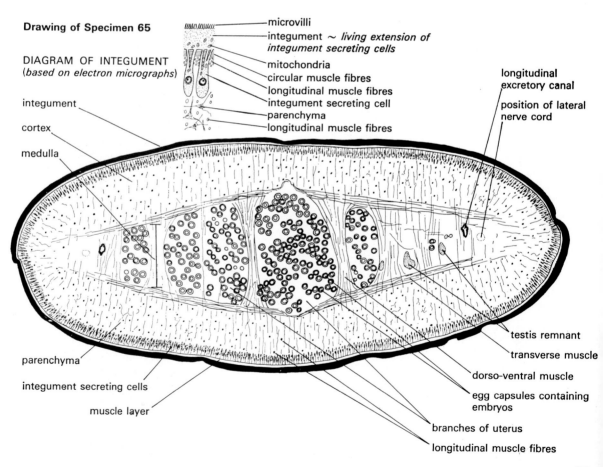

Drawing of Specimen 66

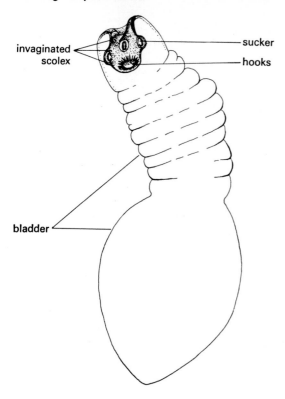

invaginated
scolex

sucker

hooks

bladder

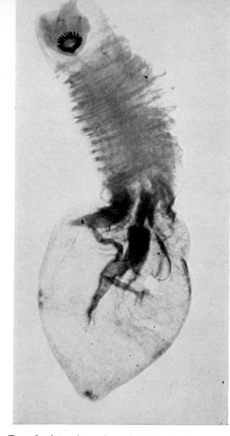

66. *Taenia,* invaginated cysticercus E. Mag. ×10

67. *Taenia,* evaginated cysticerus E. Mag. ×10

Drawing of Specimen 67

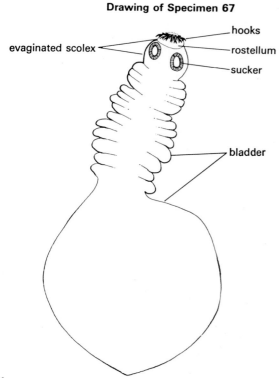

evaginated scolex

hooks

rostellum

sucker

bladder

31

68. *Ascaris,* general disse
preserved specimen. Mag.

Drawing of Specimen 68

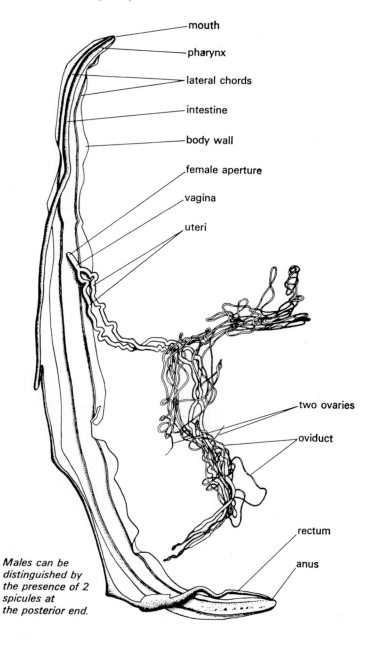

mouth

pharynx

lateral chords

intestine

body wall

female aperture

vagina

uteri

two ovaries

oviduct

rectum

anus

Males can be distinguished by the presence of 2 spicules at the posterior end.

33

Drawing of Specimen 69

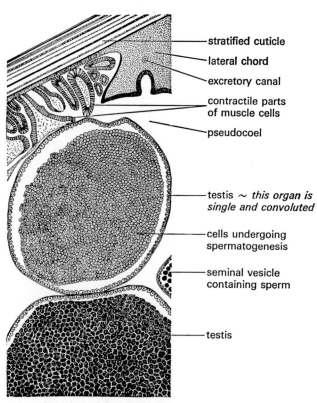

lateral nerve cord

cuticle
syncytial epidermis
muscle cell
dorsal chord
nerve cord
non-contractile part of muscle cell
pharynx
cuticle lining lumen of pharynx
marginal fibres
glandular tissue
radial muscle fibres
lateral chord
pseudocoel
ventral chord

excretory duct

69. *Ascaris*, pharyngeal region TS. Mag. ×40

70. *Ascaris*, body region TS. Mag. ×200

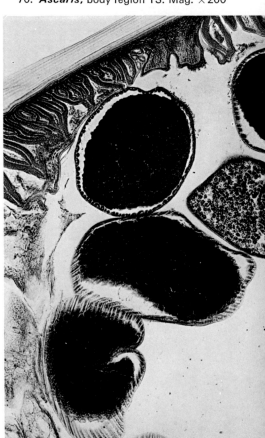

stratified cuticle
lateral chord
excretory canal
contractile parts of muscle cells
pseudocoel
testis ~ *this organ is single and convoluted*
cells undergoing spermatogenesis
seminal vesicle containing sperm
testis

Drawing of Specimen 70

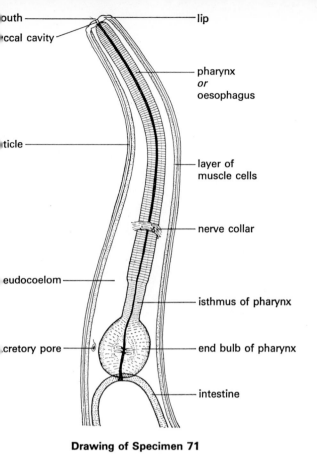

mouth —— lip

ccal cavity

pharynx
or
oesophagus

ticle ——

layer of
muscle cells

nerve collar

eudocoelom ——

isthmus of pharynx

cretory pore ——

end bulb of pharynx

intestine

Drawing of Specimen 71

72. *Trichinella*, encysted larvae E. Mag. ×175

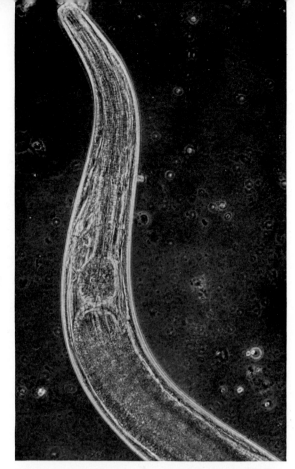

71. **Nematode,** living, phase contrast. Mag. ×275

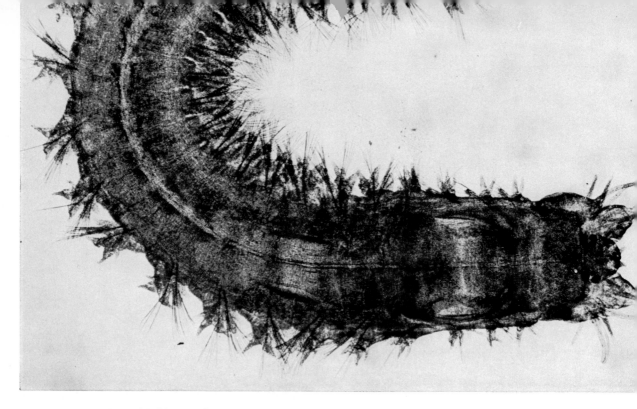

73. *Nereis,* anterior end E. Mag. ×15

74. *Nereis,* TS. Mag. ×45

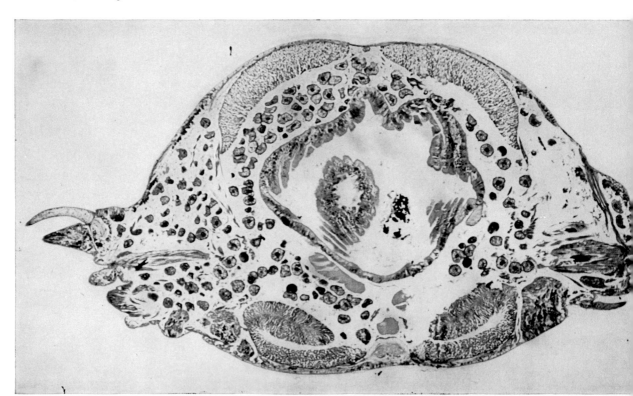

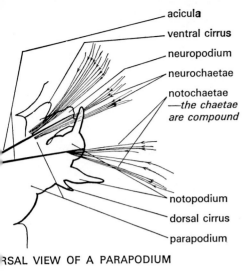

acicula
ventral cirrus
neuropodium
neurochaetae
notochaetae
—*the chaetae
are compound*

notopodium
dorsal cirrus
parapodium

RSAL VIEW OF A PARAPODIUM

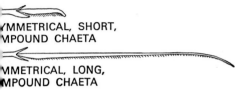

YMMETRICAL, SHORT,
MPOUND CHAETA

MMETRICAL, LONG,
MPOUND CHAETA

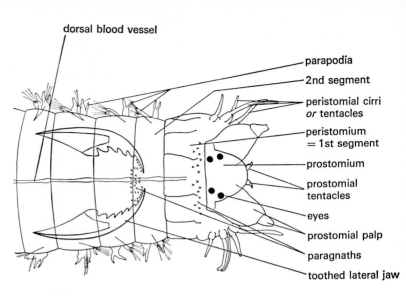

dorsal blood vessel

parapodia
2nd segment
peristomial cirri *or* tentacles
peristomium = 1st segment
prostomium
prostomial tentacles
eyes
prostomial palp
paragnaths
toothed lateral jaw

DRAWING OF THE FIRST FIVE SEGMENTS

Drawing of Specimen 73

Drawing of Specimen 74

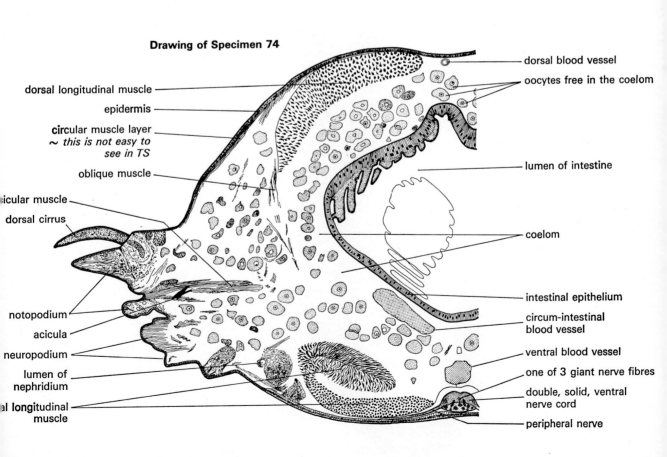

dorsal longitudinal muscle
epidermis
circular muscle layer
~ *this is not easy to
see in TS*
oblique muscle

icular muscle
dorsal cirrus

notopodium
acicula
neuropodium
lumen of nephridium
al longitudinal muscle

dorsal blood vessel
oocytes free in the coelom

lumen of intestine

coelom

intestinal epithelium
circum-intestinal blood vessel
ventral blood vessel
one of 3 giant nerve fibres
double, solid, ventral nerve cord
peripheral nerve

75. *Arenicola,* general dissection,
fresh specimen. Mag. ×2

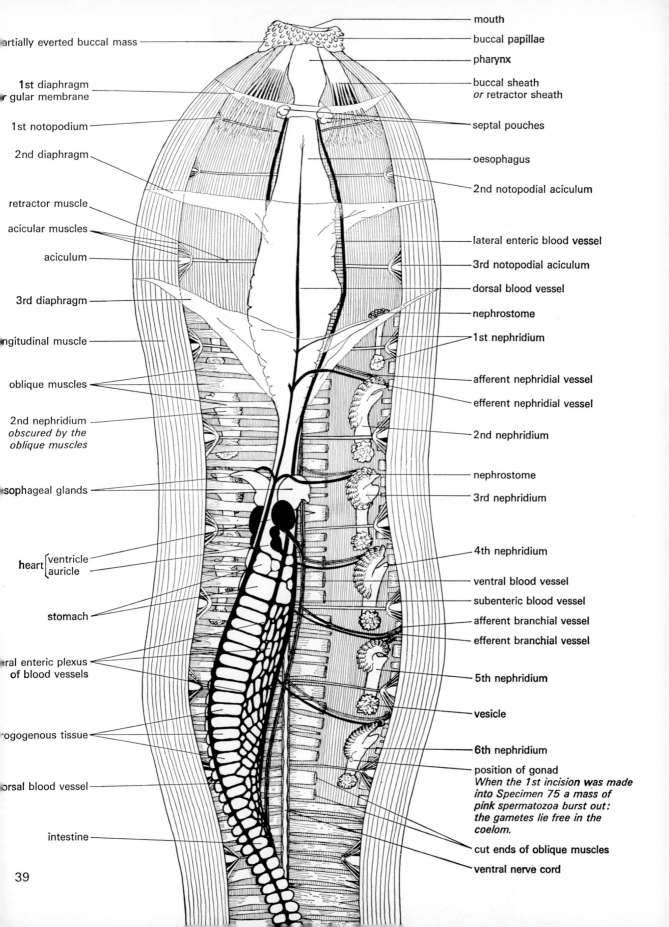

mouth

buccal **papillae**

pharynx

artially everted buccal mass

buccal sheath
or retractor sheath

1st diaphragm
r gular membrane

1st notopodium

septal pouches

2nd diaphragm

oesophagus

2nd notopodial aciculum

retractor muscle

acicular muscles

aciculum

lateral enteric blood **vessel**

3rd notopodial aciculum

dorsal blood vessel

3rd diaphragm

nephrostome

1st nephridium

ngitudinal muscle

oblique muscles

afferent nephridial **vessel**

efferent nephridial **vessel**

2nd nephridium
*obscured by the
oblique muscles*

2nd nephridium

nephrostome

3rd nephridium

sophageal glands

heart $\begin{cases}$ ventricle \\ auricle $\end{cases}$

4th nephridium

ventral blood vessel

subenteric blood vessel

afferent branchial vessel

efferent branchial vessel

stomach

ral enteric plexus
of blood vessels

5th nephridium

vesicle

rogogenous tissue

6th nephridium

position of gonad
*When the 1st incision was made
into Specimen 75 a mass of
pink spermatozoa burst out:
the gametes lie free in the
coelom.*

orsal blood vessel

cut ends of oblique muscles

ventral nerve cord

intestine

39

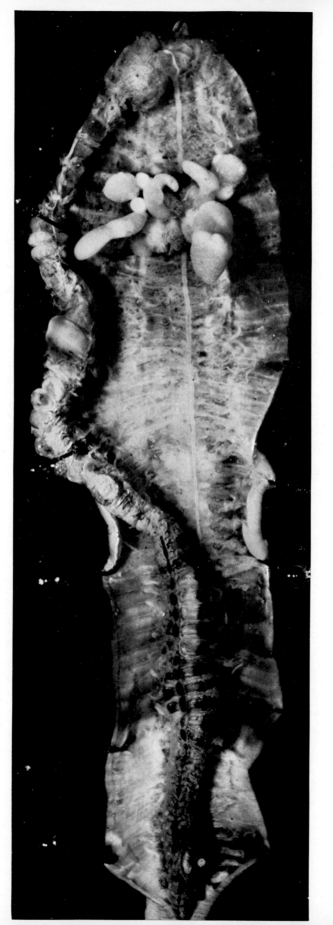

76. **Earthworm,** general dissection, fresh specimen. Mag. × 5

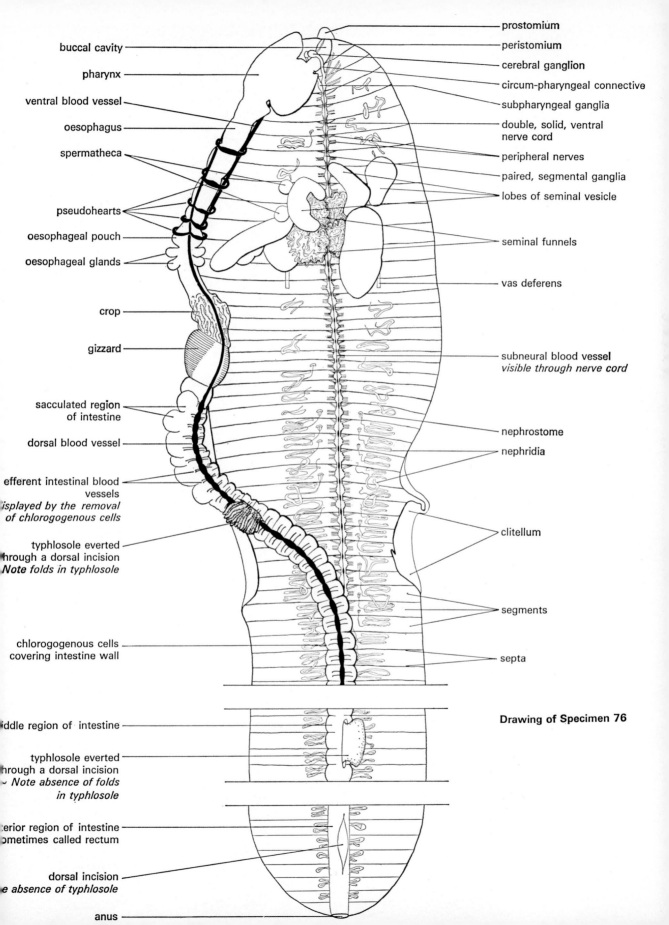

buccal cavity

pharynx

ventral blood vessel

oesophagus

spermatheca

pseudohearts

oesophageal pouch

oesophageal glands

crop

gizzard

sacculated region
of intestine

dorsal blood vessel

efferent intestinal blood
vessels
*displayed by the removal
of chlorogogenous cells*

typhlosole everted
*through a dorsal incision
Note folds in typhlosole*

chlorogogenous cells
covering intestine wall

prostomium

peristomium

cerebral ganglion

circum-pharyngeal connective

subpharyngeal ganglia

double, solid, ventral
nerve cord

peripheral nerves

paired, segmental ganglia

lobes of seminal vesicle

seminal funnels

vas deferens

subneural blood vessel
visible through nerve cord

nephrostome

nephridia

clitellum

segments

septa

Middle region of intestine

typhlosole everted
*through a dorsal incision
Note absence of folds
in typhlosole*

Posterior region of intestine
sometimes called rectum

dorsal incision
Note absence of typhlosole

anus

Drawing of Specimen 76

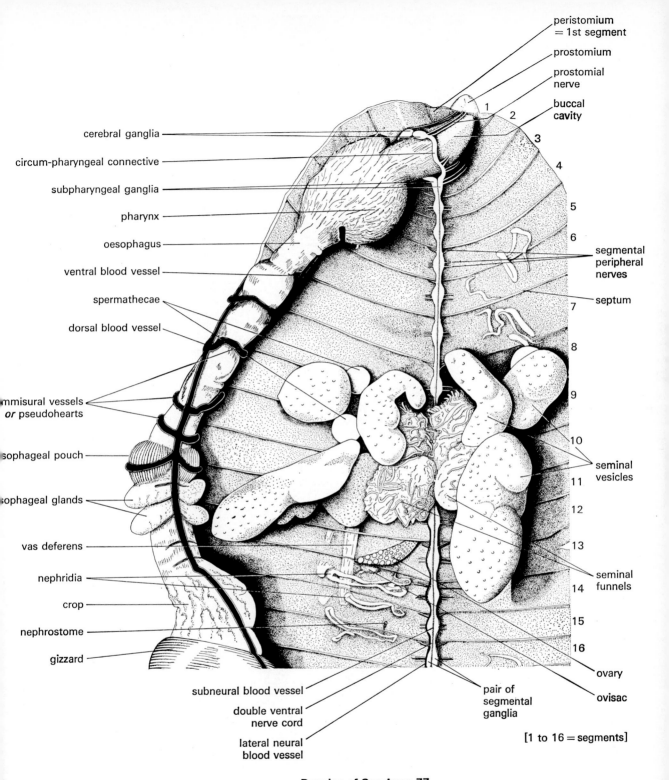

peristomium = 1st segment

prostomium

prostomial nerve

buccal cavity

cerebral ganglia

circum-pharyngeal connective

subpharyngeal ganglia

pharynx

oesophagus

ventral blood vessel

spermathecae

dorsal blood vessel

commisural vessels *or* pseudohearts

oesophageal pouch

oesophageal glands

vas deferens

nephridia

crop

nephrostome

gizzard

segmental peripheral nerves

septum

seminal vesicles

seminal funnels

ovary

ovisac

1
2
3
4
5
6
7
8
9
10
11
12
13
14
15
16

subneural blood vessel

double ventral nerve cord

lateral neural blood vessel

pair of segmental ganglia

[1 to 16 = segments]

Drawing of Specimen 77

77. **Earthworm,** dissection of anterior end, fresh specimen. Mag. ×15

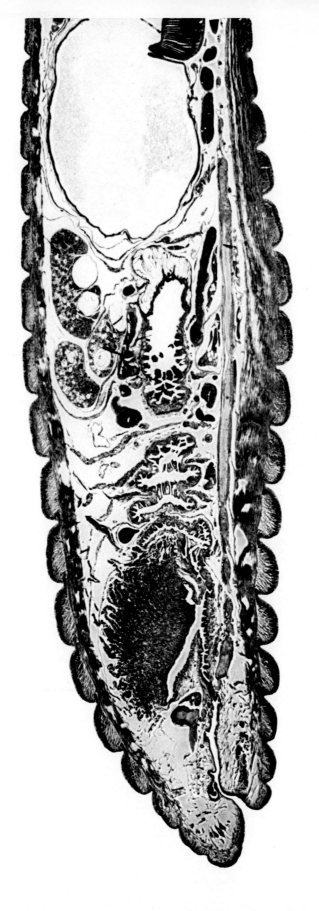

78. *Lumbricus*, median LS anterior end. Mag. ×14

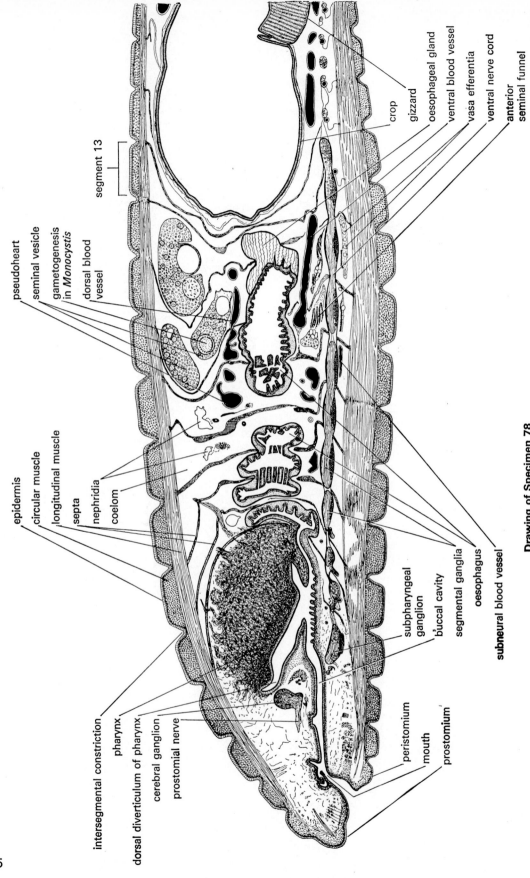

segment 13

pseudoheart
seminal vesicle
gametogenesis
in *Monocystis*
dorsal blood
vessel

epidermis
circular muscle
longitudinal muscle
septa
nephridia
coelom

intersegmental constriction
pharynx
dorsal diverticulum of pharynx
cerebral ganglion
prostomial nerve

crop
gizzard
oesophageal gland
ventral blood vessel
vasa efferentia
ventral nerve cord
**anterior
seminal funnel**

subpharyngeal
ganglion
buccal cavity
segmental ganglia
oesophagus
subneural blood vessel

peristomium
mouth
prostomium

Drawing of Specimen 78

45

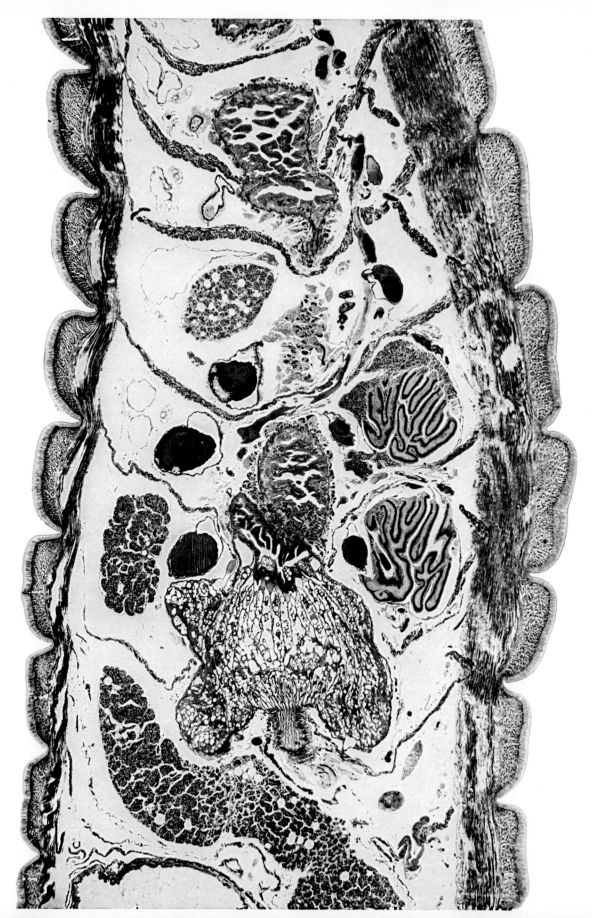

79. **Lumbricus,** reproductive region LS. Mag. ×30

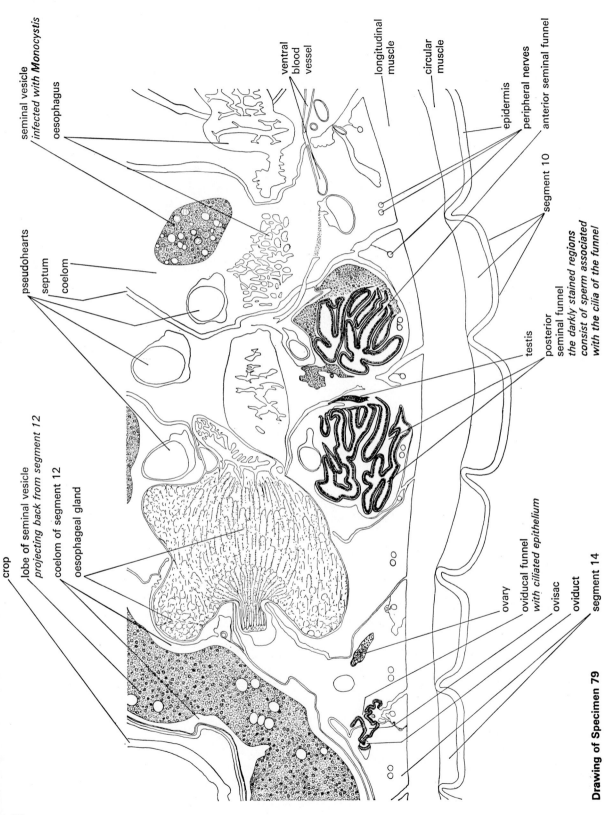

seminal vesicle
infected with **Monocystis**
oesophagus

ventral
blood
vessel

longitudinal
muscle

circular
muscle

epidermis
peripheral nerves
anterior seminal funnel

segment 10

pseudohearts
septum
coelom

testis

posterior
seminal funnel
*the darkly stained regions
consist of sperm associated
with the cilia of the funnel*

crop
lobe of seminal vesicle
projecting back from segment 12
coelom of segment 12
oesophageal gland

ovary
oviducal funnel
with ciliated epithelium
ovisac
oviduct
segment 14

Drawing of Specimen 79

47

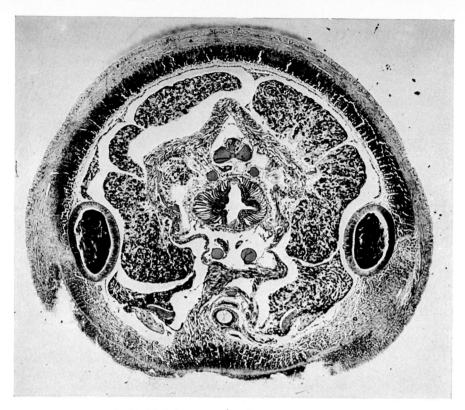

80. **Lumbricus,** œsophageal region TS. Mag. ×25

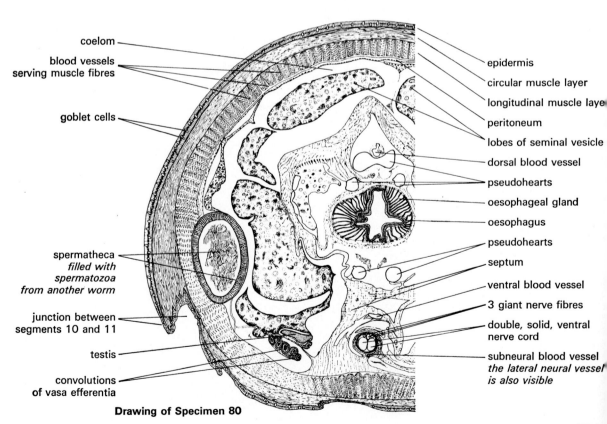

coelom

blood vessels
serving muscle fibres

goblet cells

spermatheca
*filled with
spermatozoa
from another worm*

junction between
segments 10 and 11

testis

convolutions
of vasa efferentia

epidermis

circular muscle layer

longitudinal muscle layer

peritoneum

lobes of seminal vesicle

dorsal blood vessel

pseudohearts

oesophageal gland

oesophagus

pseudohearts

septum

ventral blood vessel

3 giant nerve fibres

double, solid, ventral
nerve cord

subneural blood vessel
*the lateral neural vessel
is also visible*

Drawing of Specimen 80

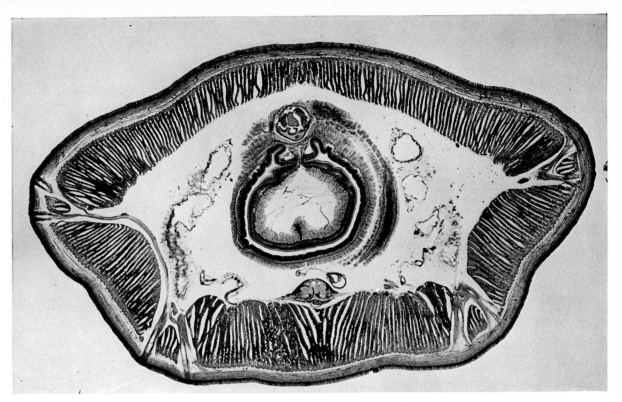

81. *Lumbricus,* intestinal region TS. Mag. ×24

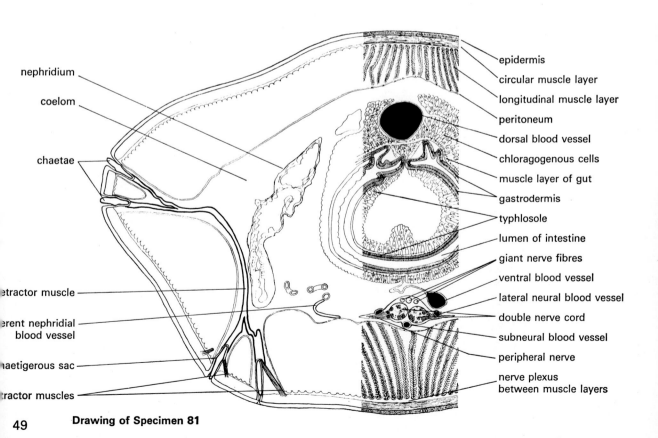

nephridium

coelom

chaetae

epidermis

circular muscle layer

longitudinal muscle layer

peritoneum

dorsal blood vessel

chloragogenous cells

muscle layer of gut

gastrodermis

typhlosole

lumen of intestine

giant nerve fibres

ventral blood vessel

lateral neural blood vessel

double nerve cord

subneural blood vessel

peripheral nerve

nerve plexus
between muscle layers

etractor muscle

erent nephridial
blood vessel

naetigerous sac

tractor muscles

Drawing of Specimen 81

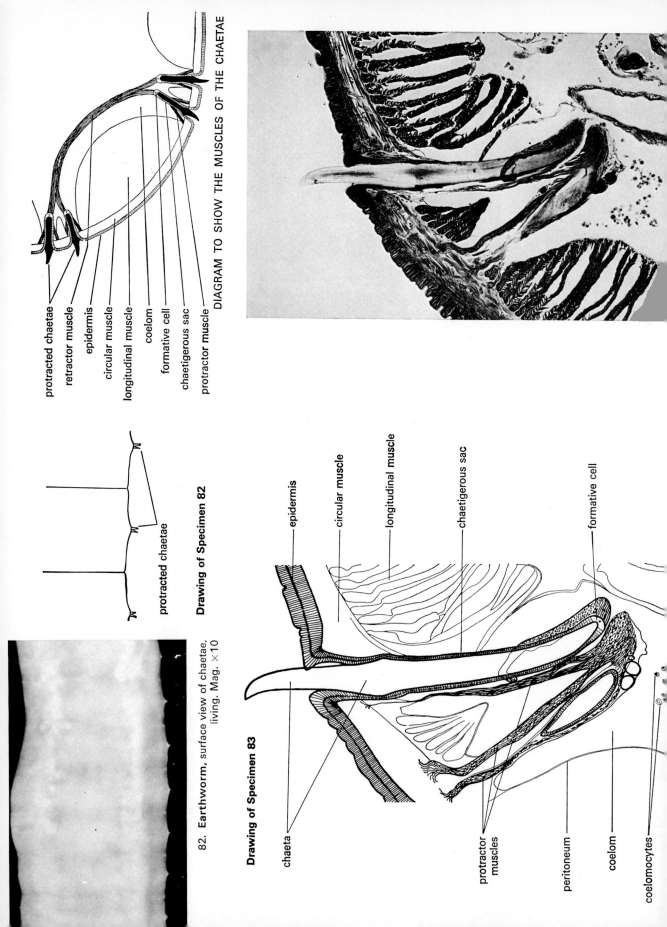

protracted chaetae
retractor muscle
epidermis
circular muscle
longitudinal muscle
coelom
formative cell
chaetigerous sac
protractor muscle

DIAGRAM TO SHOW THE MUSCLES OF THE CHAETAE

protracted chaetae

Drawing of Specimen 82

82. **Earthworm,** surface view of chaetae, living. Mag. ×10

Drawing of Specimen 83

epidermis
circular muscle
longitudinal muscle
chaetigerous sac
formative cell

chaeta

protractor muscles

peritoneum

coelom

coelomocytes

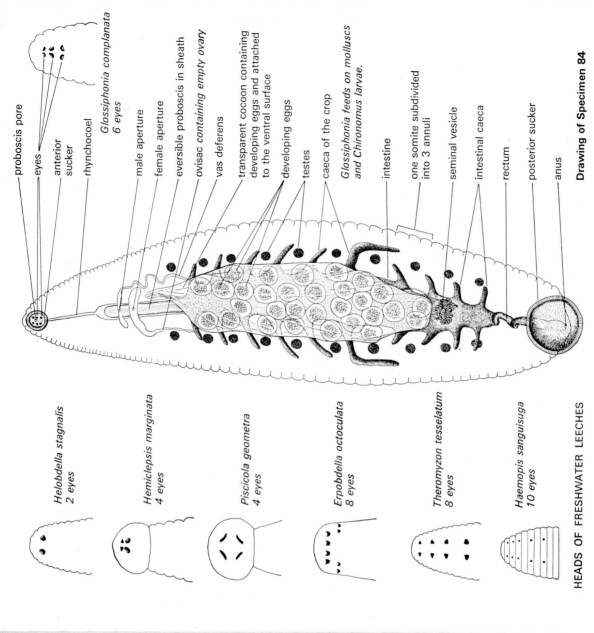

proboscis pore

eyes

anterior sucker

rhynchocoel

Glossiphonia complanata
6 eyes

male aperture

female aperture

eversible proboscis in sheath

ovisac containing empty ovary

vas deferens

transparent cocoon containing
developing eggs and attached
to the ventral surface

developing eggs

testes

caeca of the crop

*Glossiphonia feeds on molluscs
and Chironomus larvae.*

intestine

one somite subdivided
into 3 annuli

seminal vesicle

intestinal caeca

rectum

posterior sucker

anus

Drawing of Specimen 84

Helobdella stagnalis
2 eyes

Hemiclepsis marginata
4 eyes

Piscicola geometra
4 eyes

Erpobdella octoculata
8 eyes

Theromyzon tesselatum
8 eyes

Haemopis sanguisuga
10 eyes

HEADS OF FRESHWATER LEECHES

84. *Glossiphonia*, E. Mag. ×10

51

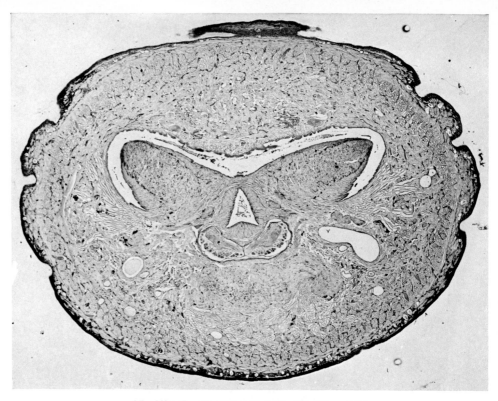

85. *Hirudo,* œsophageal region TS. Mag. ×12

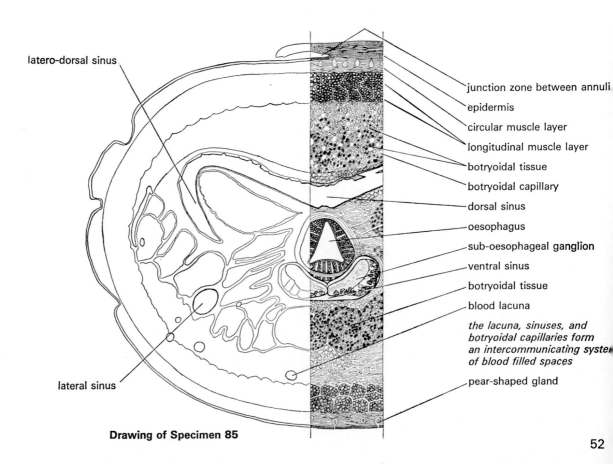

latero-dorsal sinus

junction zone between annuli

epidermis

circular muscle layer

longitudinal muscle layer

botryoidal tissue

botryoidal capillary

dorsal sinus

oesophagus

sub-oesophageal ganglion

ventral sinus

botryoidal tissue

blood lacuna

*the lacuna, sinuses, and
botryoidal capillaries form
an intercommunicating system
of blood filled spaces*

pear-shaped gland

lateral sinus

Drawing of Specimen 85

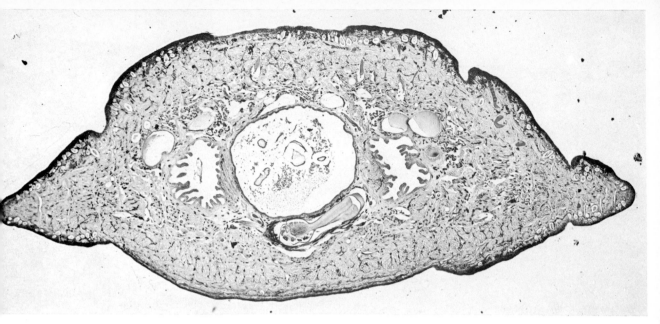

86. **Hirudo,** mid-gut region TS. Mag. ×12

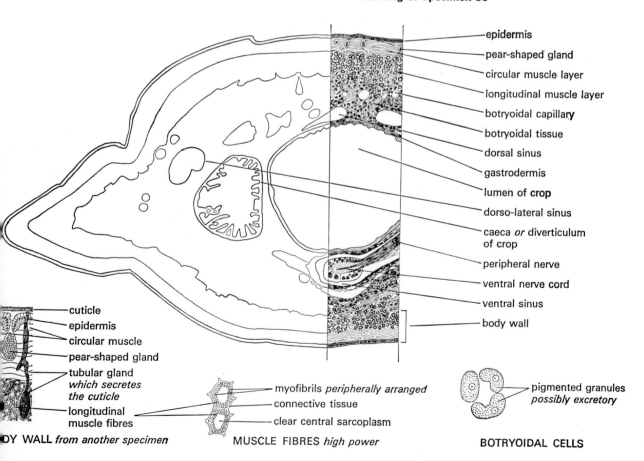

Drawing of Specimen 86

- epidermis
- pear-shaped gland
- circular muscle layer
- longitudinal muscle layer
- botryoidal capillary
- botryoidal tissue
- dorsal sinus
- gastrodermis
- lumen of crop
- dorso-lateral sinus
- caeca *or* diverticulum of crop
- peripheral nerve
- ventral nerve cord
- ventral sinus
- body wall

- cuticle
- epidermis
- circular muscle
- pear-shaped gland
- tubular gland *which secretes the cuticle*
- longitudinal muscle fibres

BODY WALL *from another specimen*

- myofibrils *peripherally arranged*
- connective tissue
- clear central sarcoplasm

MUSCLE FIBRES *high power*

- pigmented granules *possibly excretory*

BOTRYOIDAL CELLS

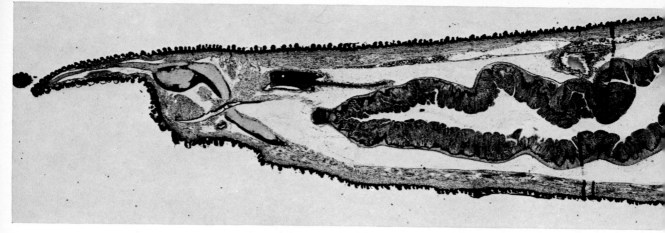

87. *Peripatus,* anterior end LS. Mag. ×20

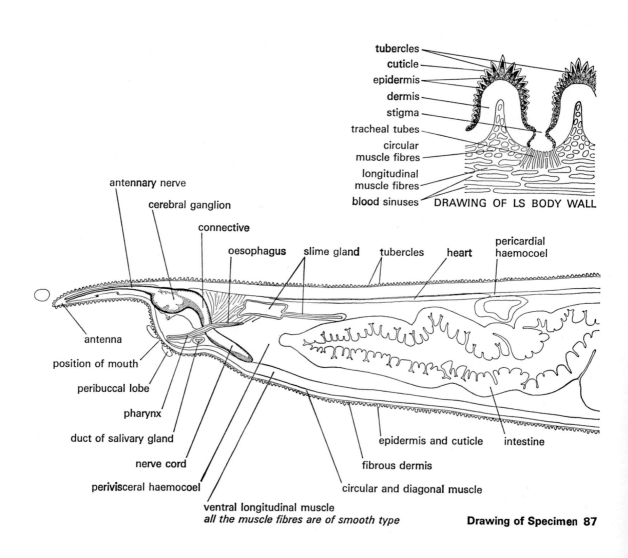

tubercles
cuticle
epidermis
dermis
stigma
tracheal tubes
circular
muscle fibres
longitudinal
muscle fibres
blood sinuses

DRAWING OF LS BODY WALL

antennary nerve
cerebral ganglion
connective
oesophagus   slime gland   tubercles   heart
pericardial
haemocoel

antenna
position of mouth
peribuccal lobe
pharynx
duct of salivary gland
nerve cord
perivisceral haemocoel
ventral longitudinal muscle
all the muscle fibres are of smooth type

epidermis and cuticle   intestine
fibrous dermis
circular and diagonal muscle

Drawing of Specimen 87

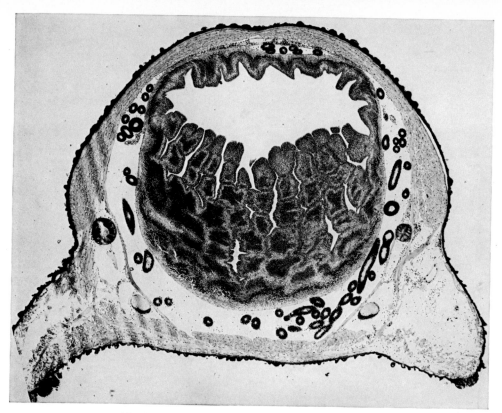

88. **Peripatus,** body and appendages TS. Mag. ×65

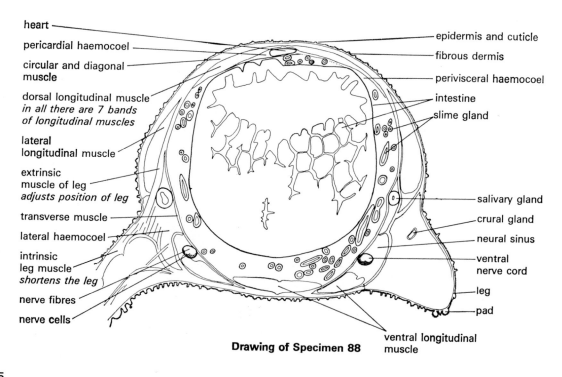

heart

pericardial haemocoel

circular and diagonal
muscle

dorsal longitudinal muscle
*in all there are 7 bands
of longitudinal muscles*

lateral
longitudinal muscle

extrinsic
muscle of leg
adjusts position of leg

transverse muscle

lateral haemocoel

intrinsic
leg muscle
shortens the leg

nerve fibres

nerve cells

epidermis and cuticle

fibrous dermis

perivisceral haemocoel

intestine

slime gland

salivary gland

crural gland

neural sinus

ventral
nerve cord

leg

pad

Drawing of Specimen 88

ventral longitudinal
muscle

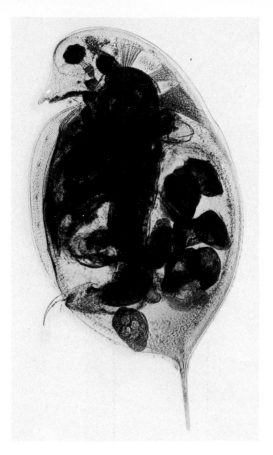

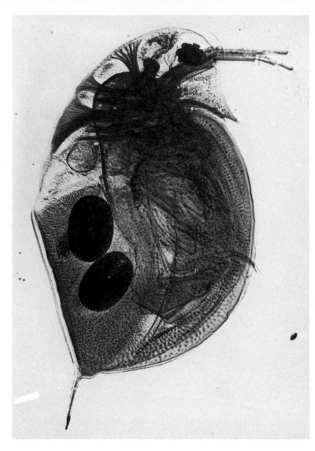

89. **Daphnia,** with 'summer' eggs, E. Mag. ×30

90. **Daphnia,** with 'winter' eggs, E. Mag. ×35

Drawing of Specimen 89

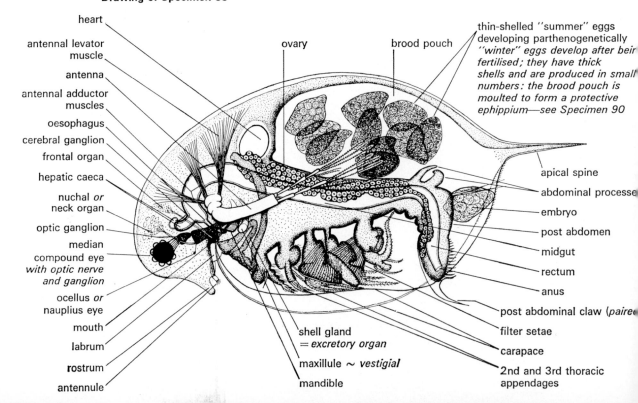

heart

antennal levator muscle

antenna

antennal adductor muscles

oesophagus

cerebral ganglion

frontal organ

hepatic caeca

nuchal *or* neck organ

optic ganglion

median compound eye *with optic nerve and ganglion*

ocellus *or* nauplius eye

mouth

labrum

rostrum

antennule

ovary

brood pouch

thin-shelled "summer" eggs developing parthenogenetically *"winter" eggs develop after being fertilised; they have thick shells and are produced in small numbers: the brood pouch is moulted to form a protective ephippium—see Specimen 90*

apical spine

abdominal processes

embryo

post abdomen

midgut

rectum

anus

post abdominal claw (paired)

filter setae

carapace

2nd and 3rd thoracic appendages

shell gland = *excretory organ*

maxillule ∼ *vestigial*

mandible

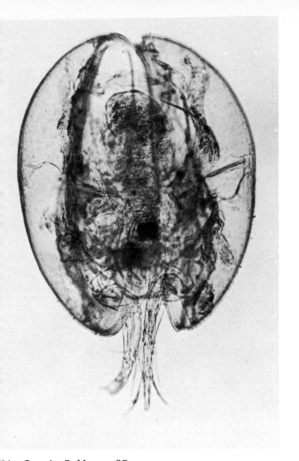

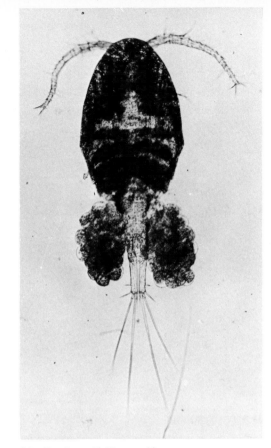

91. *Cypris*, E. Mag. ×25

92. *Cyclops*, E. Mag. ×40

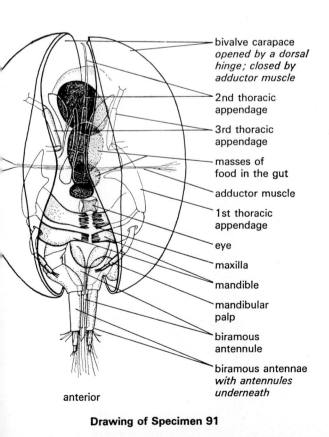

bivalve carapace
*opened by a dorsal
hinge; closed by
adductor muscle*

2nd thoracic
appendage

3rd thoracic
appendage

masses of
food in the gut

adductor muscle

1st thoracic
appendage

eye

maxilla

mandible

mandibular
palp

biramous
antennule

biramous antennae
*with antennules
underneath*

anterior

Drawing of Specimen 91

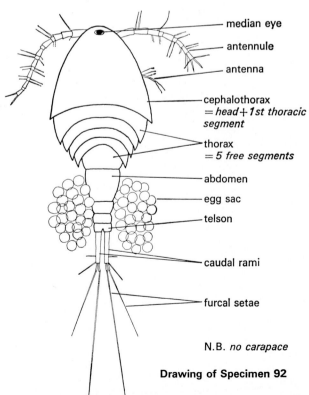

median eye

antennule

antenna

cephalothorax
*= head + 1st thoracic
segment*

thorax
= 5 free segments

abdomen

egg sac

telson

caudal rami

furcal setae

N.B. *no carapace*

Drawing of Specimen 92

Drawing of Specimen 93

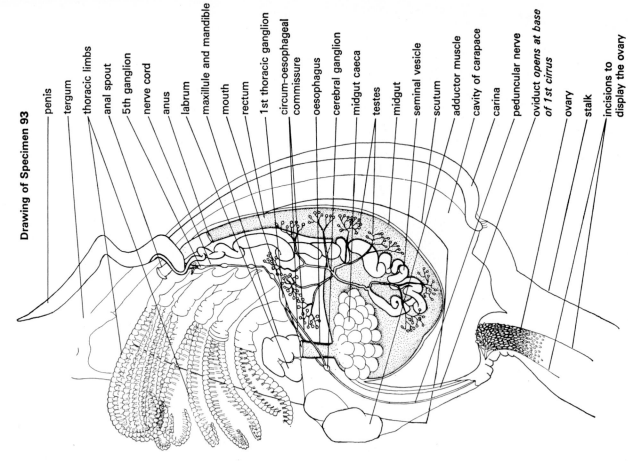

penis
tergum
thoracic limbs
anal spout
5th ganglion
nerve cord
anus
labrum
maxillule and mandible
mouth
rectum
1st thoracic ganglion
circum-oesophageal commissure
oesophagus
cerebral ganglion
midgut caeca
testes
midgut
seminal vesicle
scutum
adductor muscle
cavity of carapace
carina
peduncular nerve
oviduct *opens at base of 1st cirrus*
ovary
stalk
incisions to display the ovary

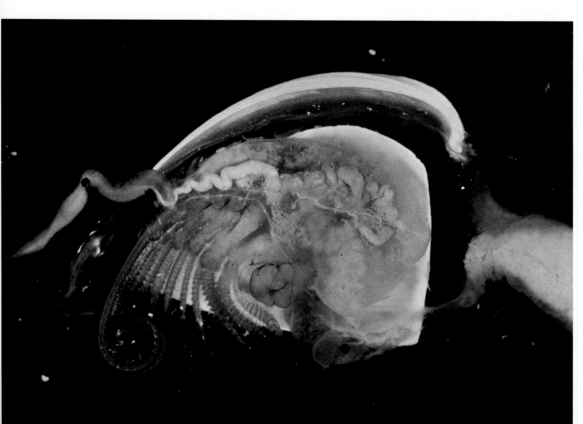

93. *Lepas*, general dissection, preserved specimen. Mag. × 4

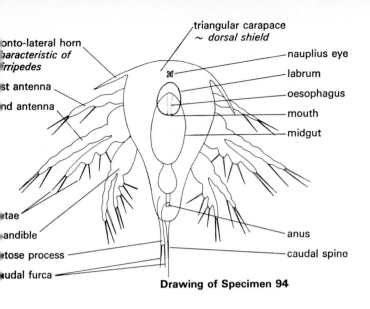

Drawing of Specimen 94

- triangular carapace ~ *dorsal shield*
- fronto-lateral horn characteristic of cirripedes
- 1st antenna
- 2nd antenna
- nauplius eye
- labrum
- oesophagus
- mouth
- midgut
- setae
- mandible
- setose process
- caudal furca
- anus
- caudal spine

94. Nauplius larvae of *Balanus*, E. Mag. ×120

Drawing of Specimen 95

- two postero-lateral carapace spines *these are 2 or 3 times the length of the body in the Anomura*
- carapace
- stalked compound eye
- rostrum
- uniramous antennules
- biramous antennae
- biramous thoracic appendages *these are the 1st and 2nd maxillipeds*
- abdomen
- rudimentary 3rd maxilliped

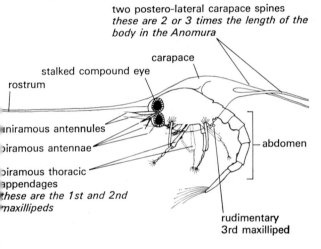

95. Zooea larva of *Porcellana*, E. Mag. ×25

96. Megalopa larva of a crab, E. Mag. ×15

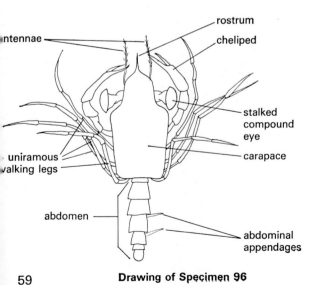

- antennae
- rostrum
- cheliped
- stalked compound eye
- carapace
- uniramous walking legs
- abdomen
- abdominal appendages

59   **Drawing of Specimen 96**

97. *Leander,* living. Mag. ×4

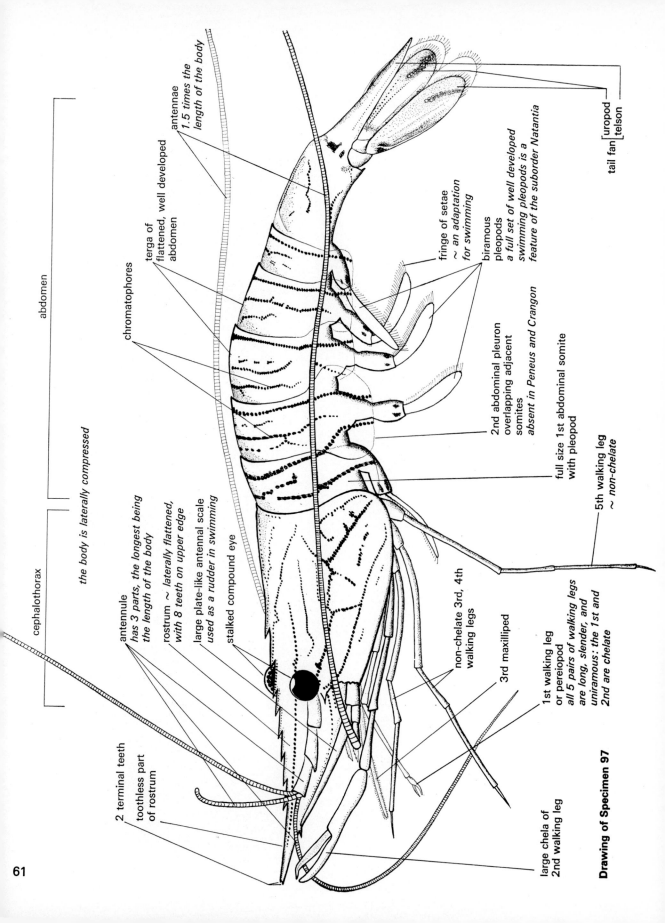

abdomen

cephalothorax

the body is laterally compressed

antennae
1.5 times the
length of the body

terga of
flattened, well developed
abdomen

chromatophores

antennule
has 3 parts, the longest being
the length of the body

rostrum ~ laterally flattened,
with 8 teeth on upper edge

large plate-like antennal scale
used as a rudder in swimming

stalked compound eye

2 terminal teeth

toothless part
of rostrum

large chela of
2nd walking leg

fringe of setae
~ an adaptation
for swimming

biramous
pleopods
a full set of well developed
swimming pleopods is a
feature of the suborder Natantia

2nd abdominal pleuron
overlapping adjacent
somites
absent in Peneus and Crangon

full size 1st abdominal somite
with pleopod

5th walking leg
~ non-chelate

uropod
telson
tail fan

non-chelate 3rd, 4th
walking legs

3rd maxilliped

1st walking leg
or pereiopod
all 5 pairs of walking legs
are long, slender, and
uniramous: the 1st and
2nd are chelate

Drawing of Specimen 97

61

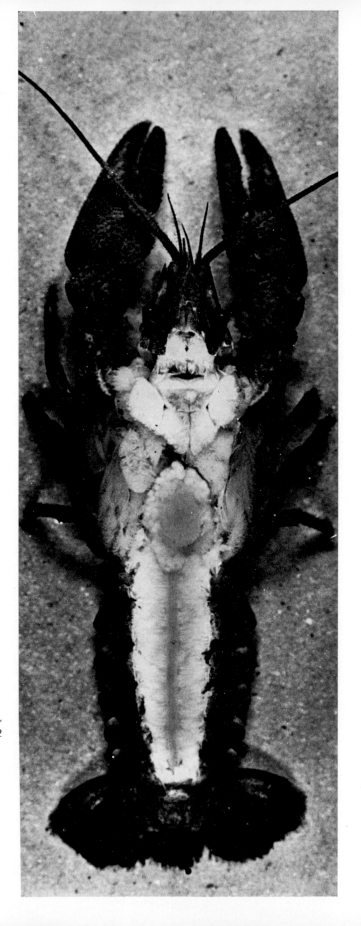

98. *Astacus,* general dissection, fresh specimen. Mag. ×2

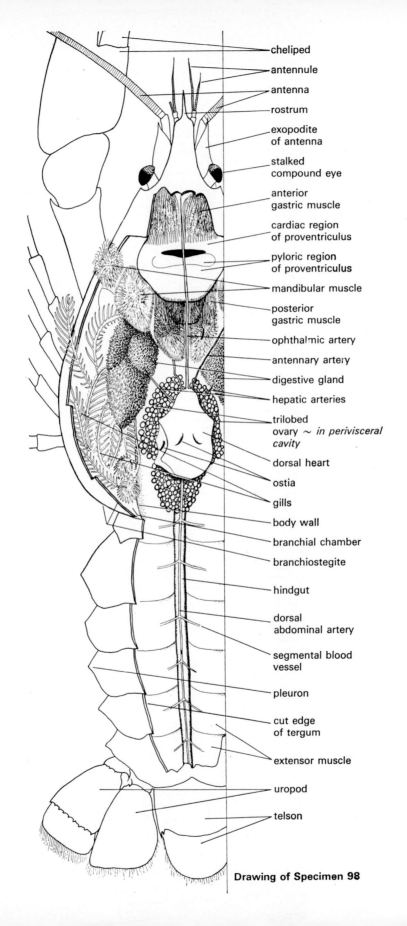

cheliped

antennule

antenna

rostrum

exopodite
of antenna

stalked
compound eye

anterior
gastric muscle

cardiac region
of proventriculus

pyloric region
of proventriculus

mandibular muscle

posterior
gastric muscle

ophthalmic artery

antennary artery

digestive gland

hepatic arteries

trilobed
ovary ~ *in perivisceral
cavity*

dorsal heart

ostia

gills

body wall

branchial chamber

branchiostegite

hindgut

dorsal
abdominal artery

segmental blood
vessel

pleuron

cut edge
of tergum

extensor muscle

uropod

telson

Drawing of Specimen 98

63

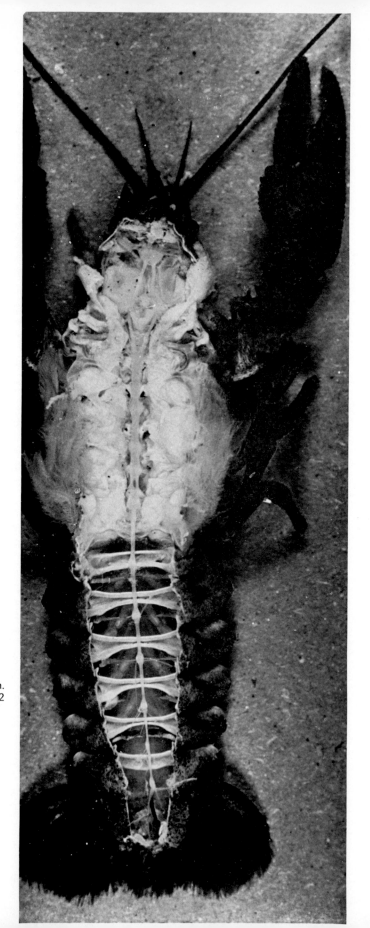

99. *Astacus*, dissection of nervous system.
Mag. ×2

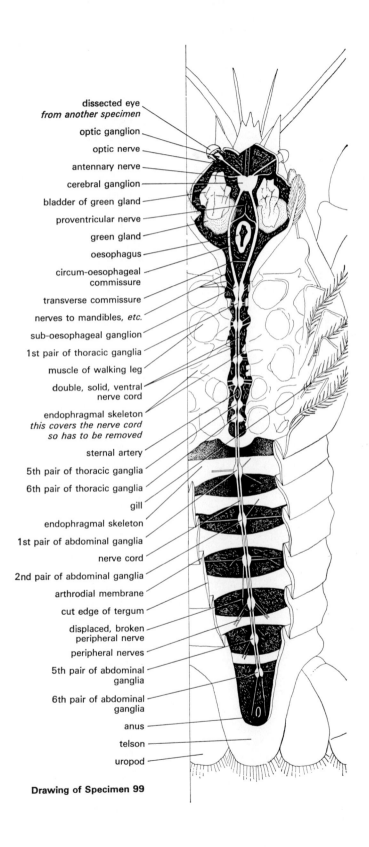

dissected eye
from another specimen
optic ganglion
optic nerve
antennary nerve
cerebral ganglion
bladder of green gland
proventricular nerve
green gland
oesophagus
circum-oesophageal
commissure
transverse commissure
nerves to mandibles, *etc.*
sub-oesophageal ganglion
1st pair of thoracic ganglia
muscle of walking leg
double, solid, ventral
nerve cord
endophragmal skeleton
*this covers the nerve cord
so has to be removed*
sternal artery
5th pair of thoracic ganglia
6th pair of thoracic ganglia
gill
endophragmal skeleton
1st pair of abdominal ganglia
nerve cord
2nd pair of abdominal ganglia
arthrodial membrane
cut edge of tergum
displaced, broken
peripheral nerve
peripheral nerves
5th pair of abdominal
ganglia
6th pair of abdominal
ganglia
anus
telson
uropod

Drawing of Specimen 99

65

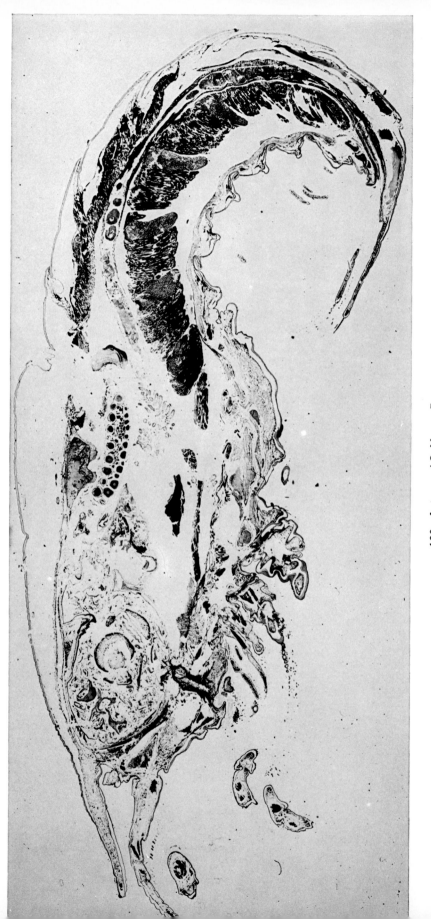

100. *Astacus,* LS. Mag. ×7

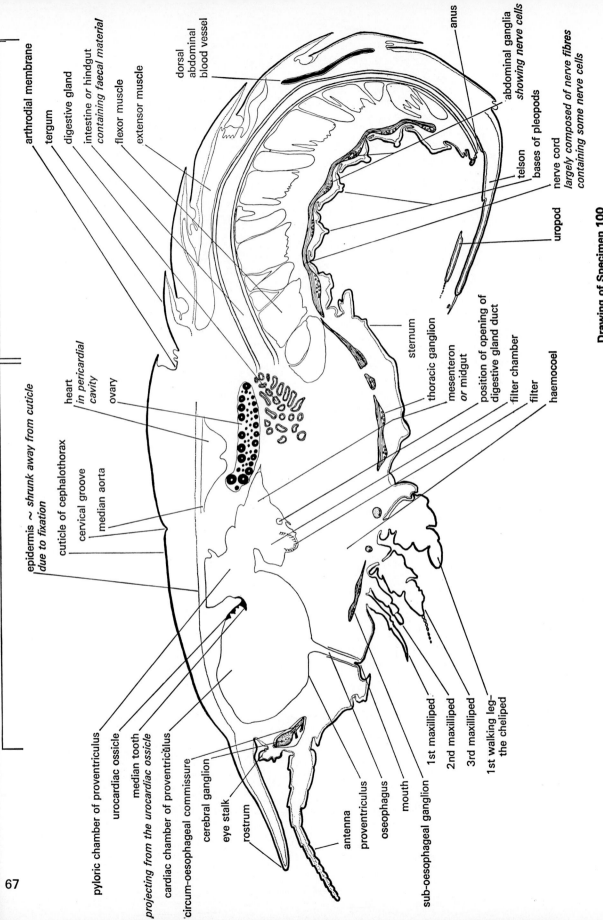

arthrodial membrane
tergum
digestive gland
intestine *or* hindgut
containing faecal material
flexor muscle
extensor muscle

dorsal
abdominal
blood vessel

anus

abdominal ganglia
showing nerve cells

telson
bases of pleopods

nerve cord
largely composed of nerve fibres
containing some nerve cells

uropod

epidermis ~ shrunk away from cuticle
due to fixation

heart
in pericardial
cavity

ovary

cuticle of cephalothorax
cervical groove
median aorta

sternum

thoracic ganglion

mesenteron
or midgut

position of opening of
digestive gland duct

filter chamber

filter

haemocoel

Drawing of Specimen 100

pyloric chamber of proventriculus
urocardiac ossicle
median tooth
projecting from the urocardiac ossicle
cardiac chamber of proventriculus
circum-oesophageal commissure
cerebral ganglion
eye stalk
rostrum

antenna
proventriculus
oseophagus
mouth
sub-oesophageal ganglion

1st maxilliped
2nd maxilliped
3rd maxilliped

1st walking leg—
the cheliped

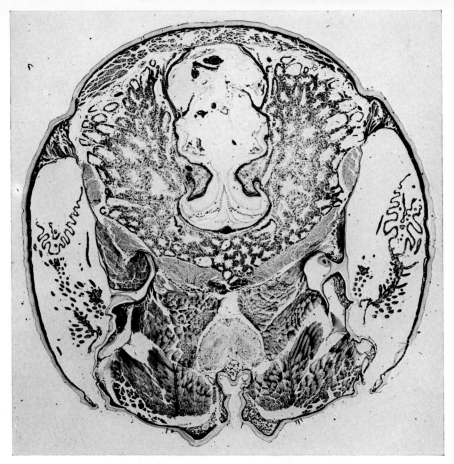

101. *Astacus*, thoracic region, TS. Mag. ×10

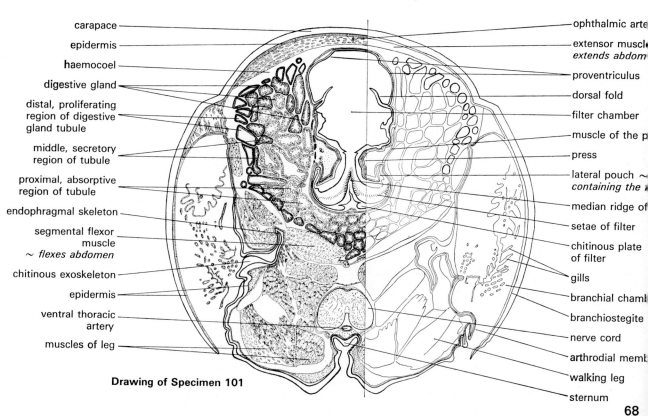

carapace

epidermis

haemocoel

digestive gland

distal, proliferating
region of digestive
gland tubule

middle, secretory
region of tubule

proximal, absorptive
region of tubule

endophragmal skeleton

segmental flexor
muscle
~ *flexes abdomen*

chitinous exoskeleton

epidermis

ventral thoracic
artery

muscles of leg

Drawing of Specimen 101

ophthalmic arte

extensor muscl
extends abdom

proventriculus

dorsal fold

filter chamber

muscle of the p

press

lateral pouch ~
containing the

median ridge of

setae of filter

chitinous plate
of filter

gills

branchial chaml

branchiostegite

nerve cord

arthrodial meml

walking leg

sternum

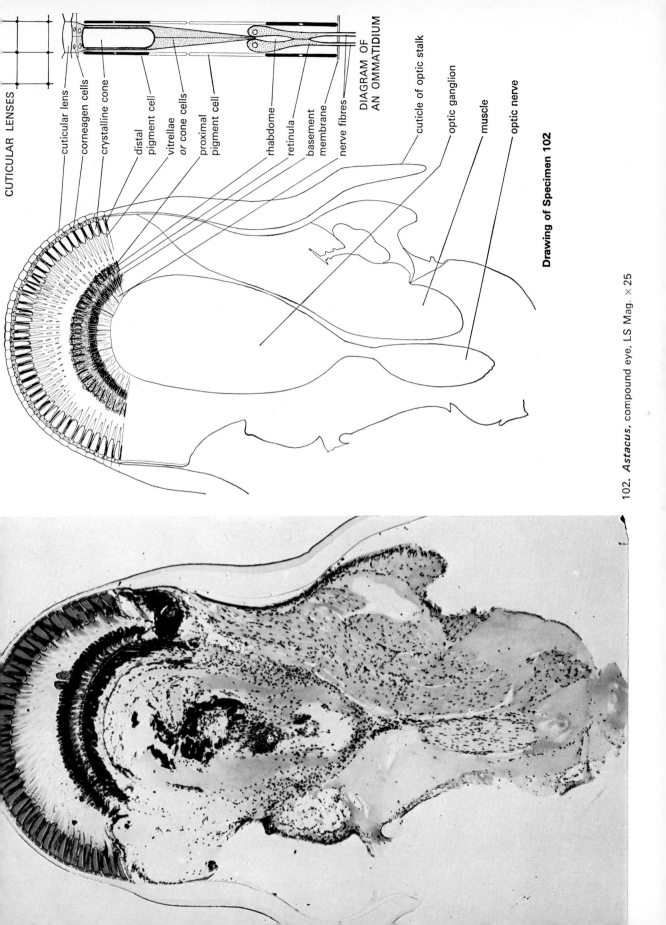

CUTICULAR LENSES

cuticular lens
corneagen cells
crystalline cone
distal
pigment cell
vitrellae
or cone cells
proximal
pigment cell
rhabdome
retinula
basement
membrane
nerve fibres

**DIAGRAM OF
AN OMMATIDIUM**

cuticle of optic stalk
optic ganglion
muscle
optic nerve

Drawing of Specimen 102

102. *Astacus,* compound eye, LS Mag. × 25

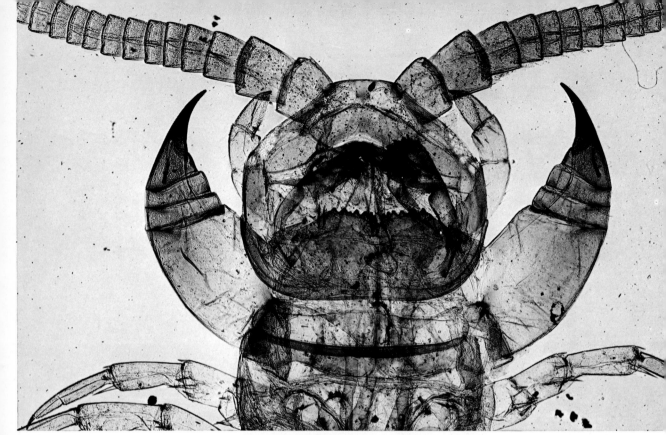

103. *Lithobius*, head, E. Mag. ×8

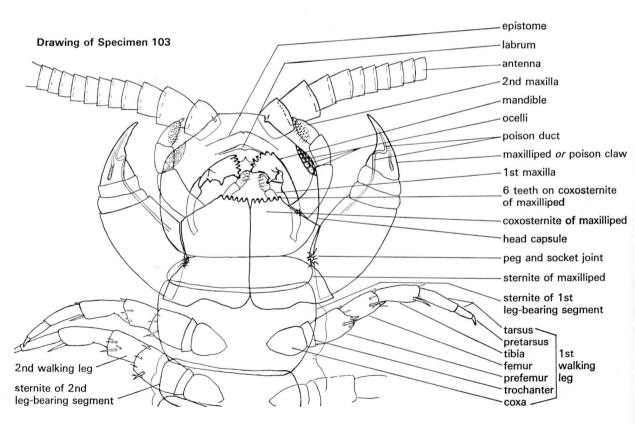

Drawing of Specimen 103

epistome
labrum
antenna
2nd maxilla
mandible
ocelli
poison duct
maxilliped *or* poison claw
1st maxilla
6 teeth on coxosternite of maxilliped
coxosternite **of** maxilliped
head capsule
peg and socket joint
sternite of maxilliped
sternite of 1st leg-bearing segment
tarsus
pretarsus
tibia
femur   1st walking leg
prefemur
trochanter
coxa

2nd walking leg
sternite of 2nd leg-bearing segment

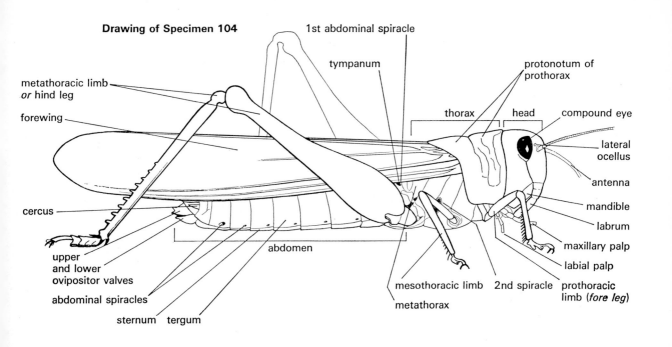

Drawing of Specimen 104

metathoracic limb *or* hind leg

forewing

1st abdominal spiracle

tympanum

protonotum of prothorax

thorax

head

compound eye

lateral ocellus

antenna

mandible

labrum

maxillary palp

labial palp

prothoracic limb (*fore leg*)

2nd spiracle

mesothoracic limb

metathorax

cercus

upper and lower ovipositor valves

abdominal spiracles

sternum   tergum

abdomen

104. *Locusta*, living. Mag. ×2

Drawing of Specimen 105

oesophagus
tracheae
salivary glands
crop
gizzard
midgut caeca
opening of caecum into midgut
midgut
malpighian tubules
pyloric valve
testis
ileum
accessory gland
vas deferens
colon
ejaculatory duct
rectum
anus
cerci

105 *Locusta*, general dissection, fresh specimen. Mag. × 3

72

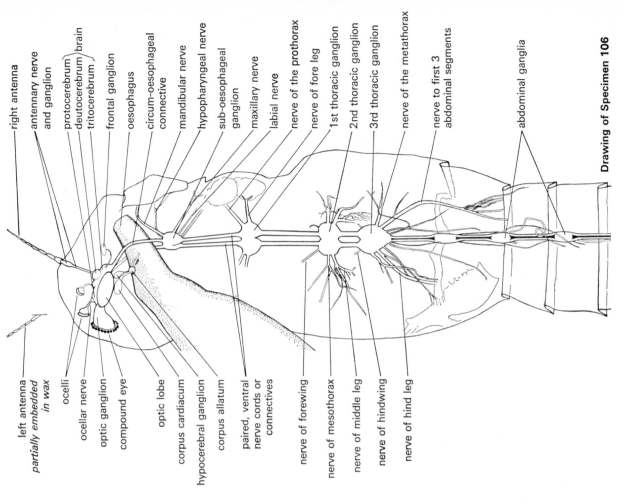

right antenna
antennary nerve
and ganglion
protocerebrum
deutocerebrum } brain
tritocerebrum
frontal ganglion
oesophagus
circum-oesophageal
connective
mandibular nerve
hypopharyngeal nerve
sub-oesophageal
ganglion
maxillary nerve
labial nerve
nerve of the prothorax
nerve of fore leg
1st thoracic ganglion
2nd thoracic ganglion
3rd thoracic ganglion
nerve of the metathorax
nerve to first 3
abdominal segments
abdominal ganglia

Drawing of Specimen 106

left antenna
*partially embedded
in wax*
ocelli
ocellar nerve
optic ganglion
compound eye
optic lobe
corpus cardiacum
hypocerebral ganglion
corpus allatum
paired, ventral
nerve cords or
connectives
nerve of forewing
nerve of mesothorax
nerve of middle leg
nerve of hindwing
nerve of hind leg

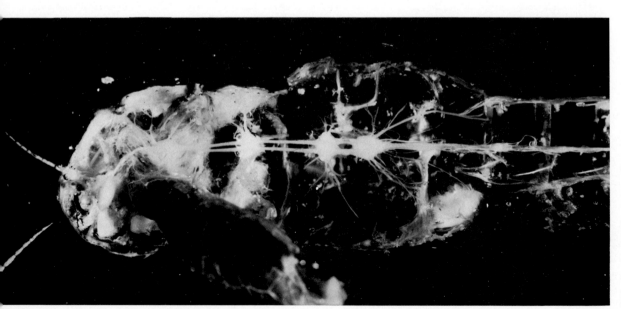

106. *Locusta*, dissection of nervous system, fresh specimen. Mag. ×5

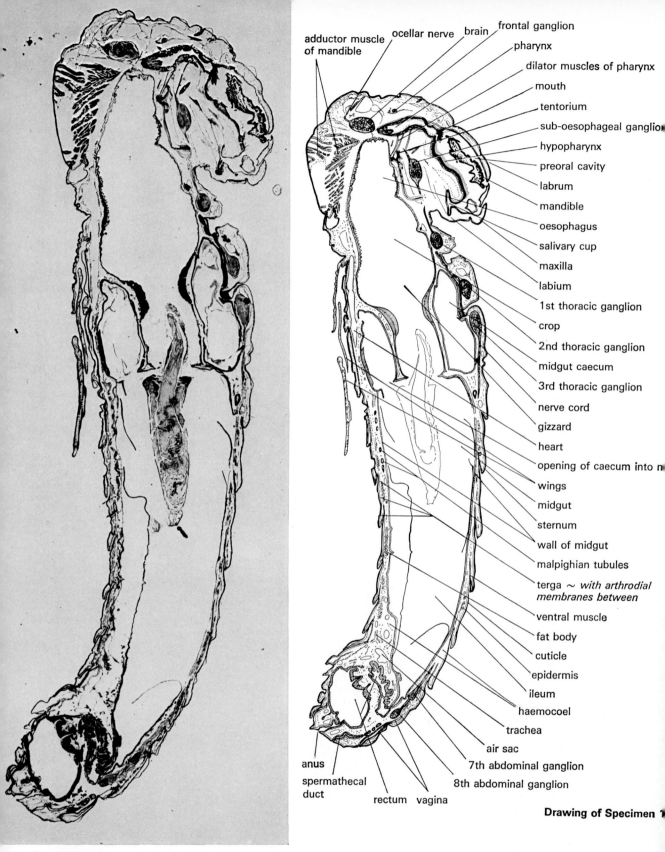

adductor muscle of mandible
ocellar nerve
brain
frontal ganglion
pharynx
dilator muscles of pharynx
mouth
tentorium
sub-oesophageal ganglion
hypopharynx
preoral cavity
labrum
mandible
oesophagus
salivary cup
maxilla
labium
1st thoracic ganglion
crop
2nd thoracic ganglion
midgut caecum
3rd thoracic ganglion
nerve cord
gizzard
heart
opening of caecum into m
wings
midgut
sternum
wall of midgut
malpighian tubules
terga ~ with arthrodial membranes between
ventral muscle
fat body
cuticle
epidermis
ileum
haemocoel
trachea
air sac
7th abdominal ganglion
8th abdominal ganglion
anus
spermathecal duct
rectum
vagina

Drawing of Specimen 1

107. *Locusta*, 4th instar nymph, LS. Mag. ×10

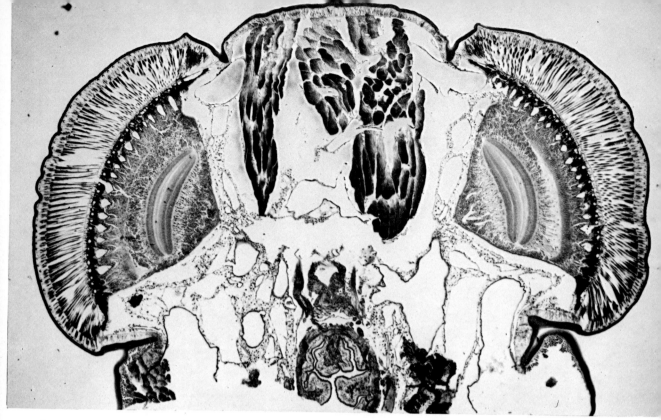

108. **Locusta**, imago, head TS. Mag. ×16

Drawing of Specimen 108

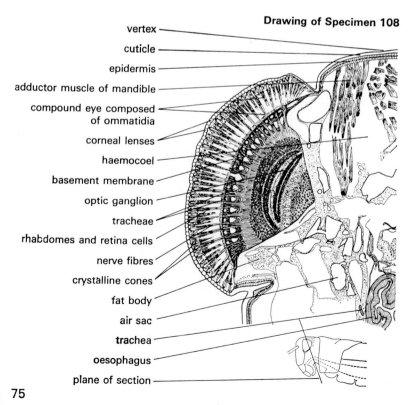

vertex
cuticle
epidermis
adductor muscle of mandible
compound eye composed of ommatidia
corneal lenses
haemocoel
basement membrane
optic ganglion
tracheae
rhabdomes and retina cells
nerve fibres
crystalline cones
fat body
air sac
trachea
oesophagus
plane of section

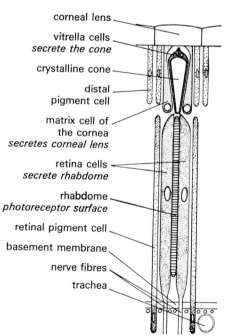

corneal lens
vitrella cells
secrete the cone
crystalline cone
distal pigment cell
matrix cell of the cornea
secretes corneal lens
retina cells
secrete rhabdome
rhabdome
photoreceptor surface
retinal pigment cell
basement membrane
nerve fibres
trachea

DIAGRAM OF AN OMMATIDIUM OF AN APPOSITION TYPE COMPOUND EYE

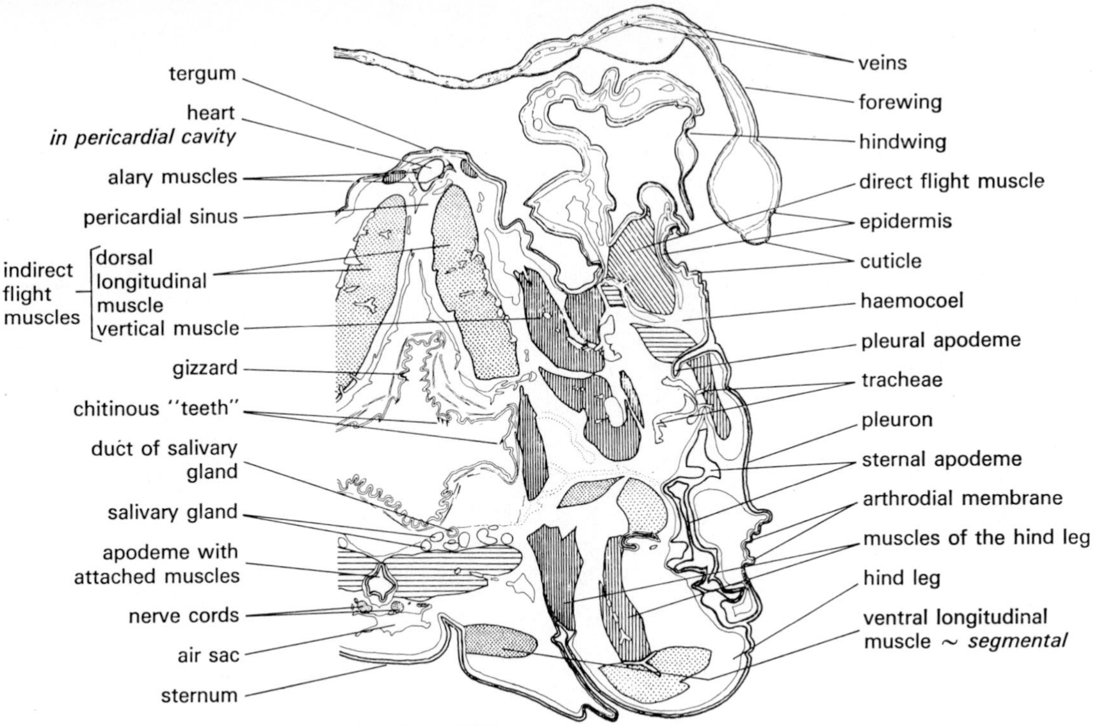
tergum
heart
in pericardial cavity
alary muscles
pericardial sinus
indirect flight muscles
dorsal longitudinal muscle
vertical muscle
gizzard
chitinous "teeth"
duct of salivary gland
salivary gland
apodeme with attached muscles
nerve cords
air sac
sternum
veins
forewing
hindwing
direct flight muscle
epidermis
cuticle
haemocoel
pleural apodeme
tracheae
pleuron
sternal apodeme
arthrodial membrane
muscles of the hind leg
hind leg
ventral longitudinal muscle ~ segmental

Drawing of Specimen 109

109. ***Locusta,*** imago, thorax TS. Mag. ×11

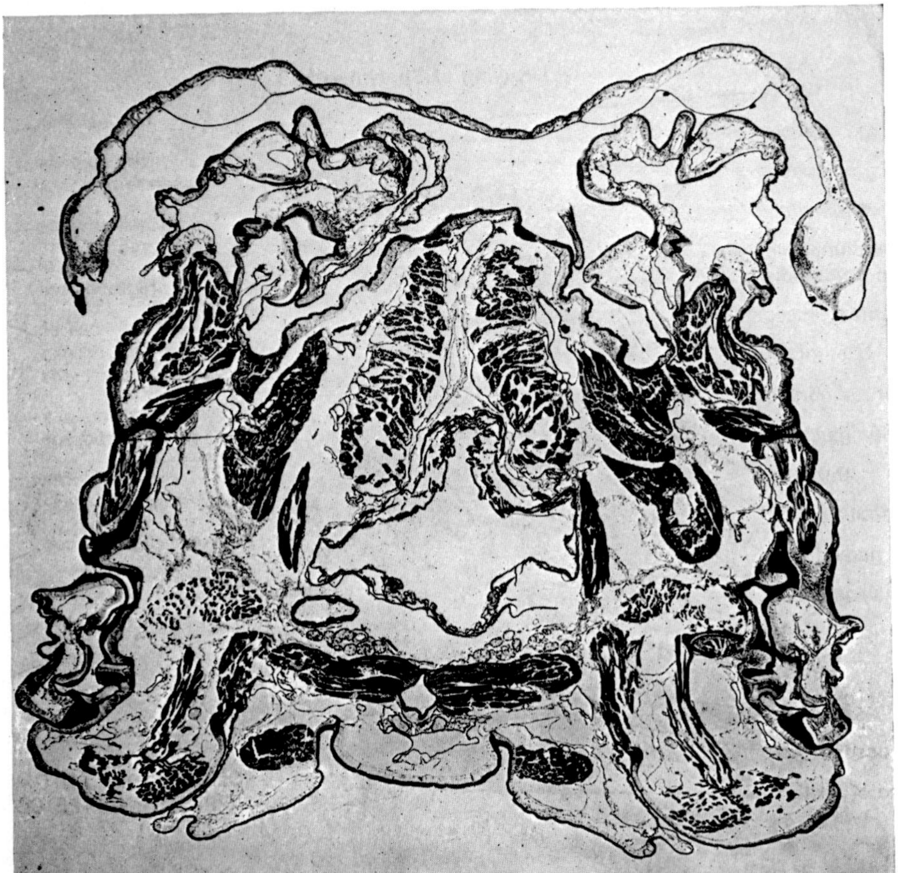

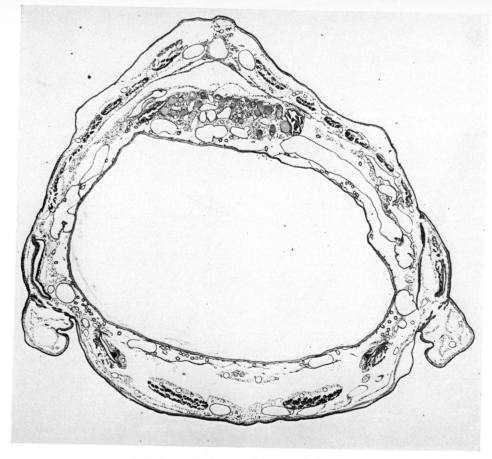

110. *Locusta*, imago, abdomen TS. Mag. ×10

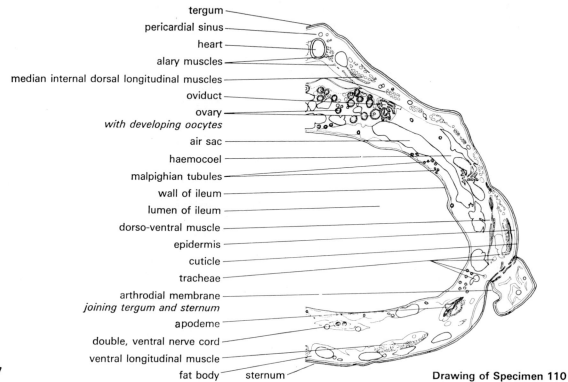

tergum

pericardial sinus

heart

alary muscles

median internal dorsal longitudinal muscles

oviduct

ovary
with developing oocytes

air sac

haemocoel

malpighian tubules

wall of ileum

lumen of ileum

dorso-ventral muscle

epidermis

cuticle

tracheae

arthrodial membrane
joining tergum and sternum

apodeme

double, ventral nerve cord

ventral longitudinal muscle

fat body   sternum

Drawing of Specimen 110

111. *Periplaneta*, mouthparts E. Mag. ×7

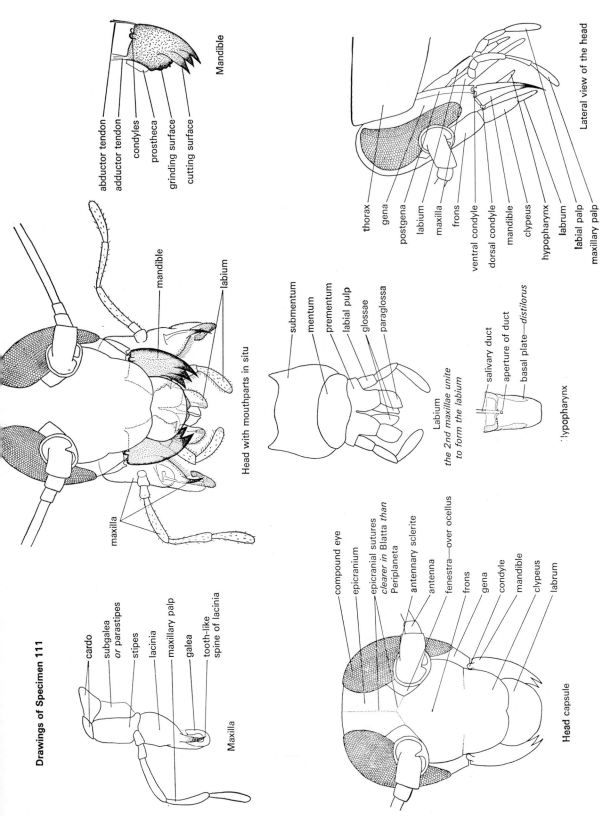

Drawings of Specimen 111

Maxilla

- cardo
- subgalea *or parastipes*
- stipes
- lacinia
- maxillary palp
- galea
- tooth-like spine of lacinia

Head with mouthparts in situ

- mandible
- labium
- maxilla

Mandible

- abductor tendon
- adductor tendon
- condyles
- prostheca
- grinding surface
- cutting surface

Labium
the 2nd maxillae unite to form the labium

- submentum
- mentum
- prementum
- labial pulp
- glossae
- paraglossa

Hypopharynx

- salivary duct
- aperture of duct
- basal plate—*distilorus*

Lateral view of the head

- thorax
- gena
- postgena
- labium
- maxilla
- frons
- ventral condyle
- dorsal condyle
- mandible
- clypeus
- hypopharynx
- labrum
- labial palp
- maxillary palp

Head capsule

- compound eye
- epicranium
- epicranial sutures *clearer in* Blatta *than* Periplaneta
- antennary sclerite
- antenna
- fenestra—over ocellus
- frons
- gena
- condyle
- mandible
- clypeus
- labrum

79

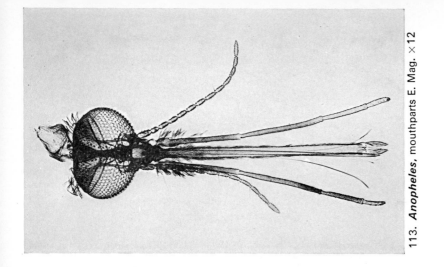

113. *Anopheles*, mouthparts E. Mag. ×12

114. Housefly, mouthparts E. Mag. ×18

112. *Apis*, worker, mouthparts E. Mag. ×10

80

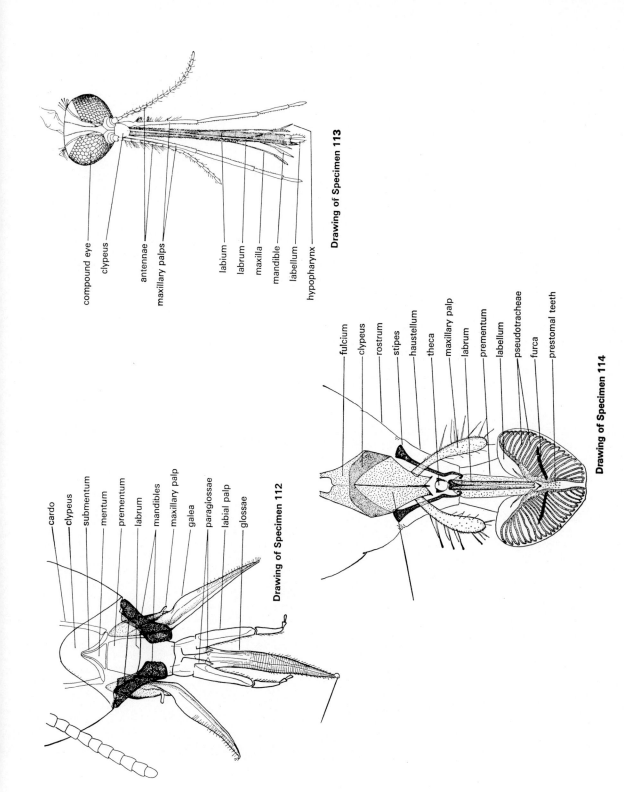

compound eye
clypeus
antennae
maxillary palps
labium
labrum
maxilla
mandible
labellum
hypopharynx

Drawing of Specimen 113

cardo
clypeus
submentum
mentum
prementum
labrum
mandibles
maxillary palp
galea
paraglossae
labial palp
glossae

Drawing of Specimen 112

fulcium
clypeus
rostrum
stipes
haustellum
theca
maxillary palp
labrum
prementum
labellum
pseudotracheae
furca
prestomal teeth

Drawing of Specimen 114

81

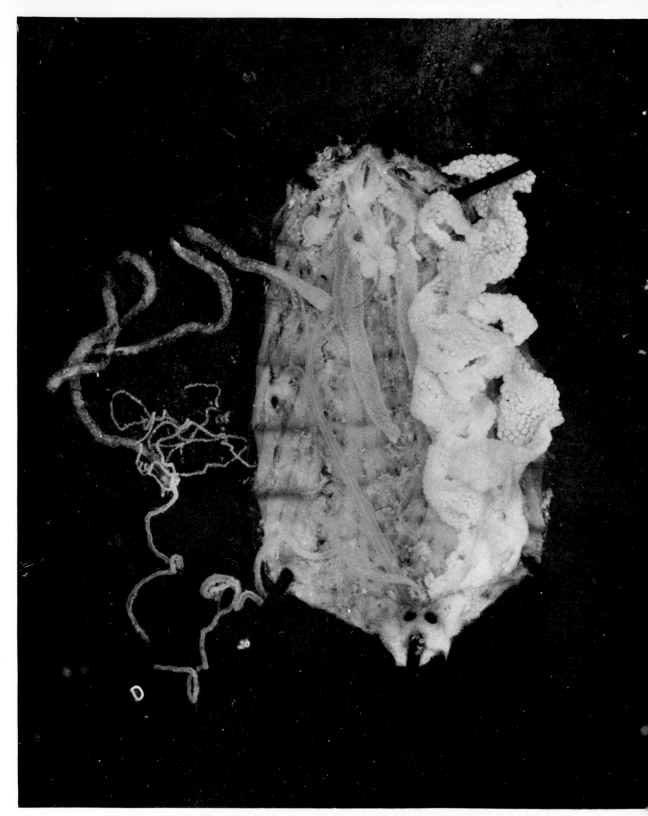

115. **Housefly,** larva, general dissection, fresh specimen. Mag. ×9

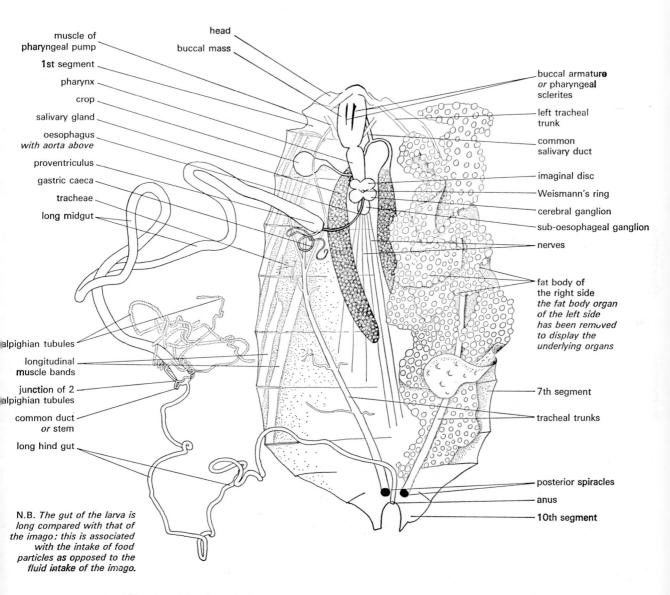

muscle of
pharyngeal pump
1st segment
pharynx
crop
salivary gland
oesophagus
with aorta above
proventriculus
gastric caeca
tracheae
long midgut

head
buccal mass

buccal armature
or pharyngeal
sclerites
left tracheal
trunk
common
salivary duct
imaginal disc
Weismann's ring
cerebral ganglion
sub-oesophageal ganglion
nerves
fat body of
the right side
*the fat body organ
of the left side
has been removed
to display the
underlying organs*

alpighian tubules
longitudinal
muscle bands
junction of 2
alpighian tubules
common duct
or stem
long hind gut

7th segment
tracheal trunks

posterior spiracles
anus
10th segment

N.B. *The gut of the larva is
long compared with that of
the imago: this is associated
with the intake of food
particles as opposed to the
fluid intake of the imago.*

Drawing of Specimen 115

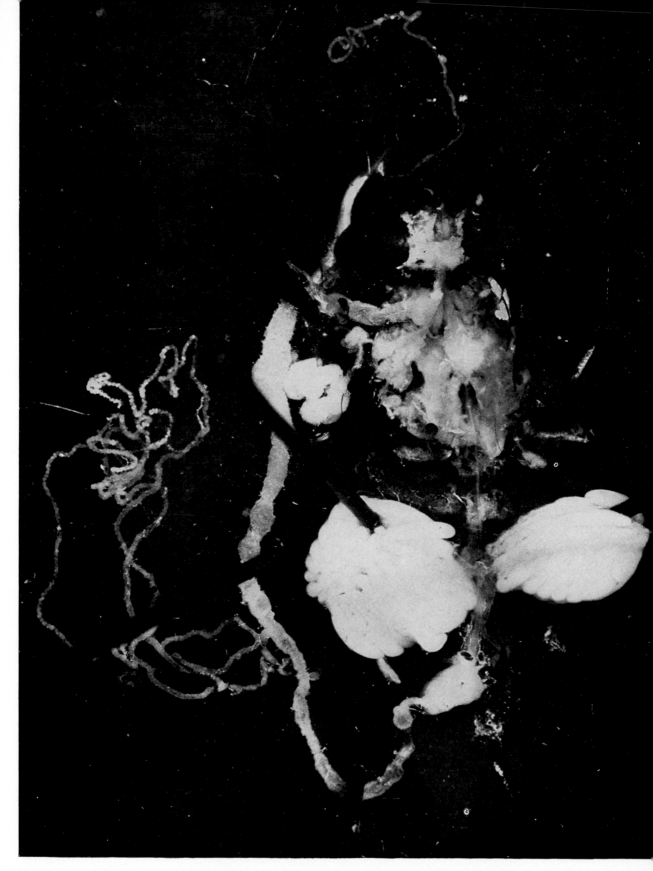

116. **Housefly,** imago, general dissection, fresh specimen. Mag. ×9

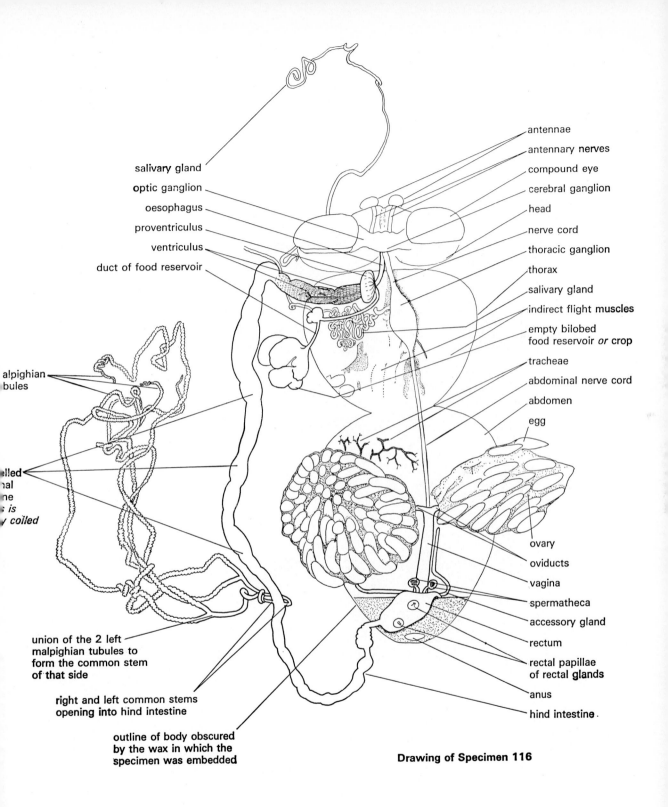

salivary gland

optic ganglion

oesophagus

proventriculus

ventriculus

duct of food reservoir

antennae

antennary nerves

compound eye

cerebral ganglion

head

nerve cord

thoracic ganglion

thorax

salivary gland

indirect flight muscles

empty bilobed
food reservoir *or* crop

tracheae

abdominal nerve cord

abdomen

egg

alpighian
bules

elled
nal
ne
s *is*
coiled

ovary

oviducts

vagina

spermatheca

accessory gland

rectum

rectal papillae
of rectal glands

anus

hind intestine

union of the 2 left
malpighian tubules to
form the common stem
of that side

right and left common stems
opening into hind intestine

outline of body obscured
by the wax in which the
specimen was embedded

Drawing of Specimen 116

85

117. **Housefly**, living imago. Mag. ×12

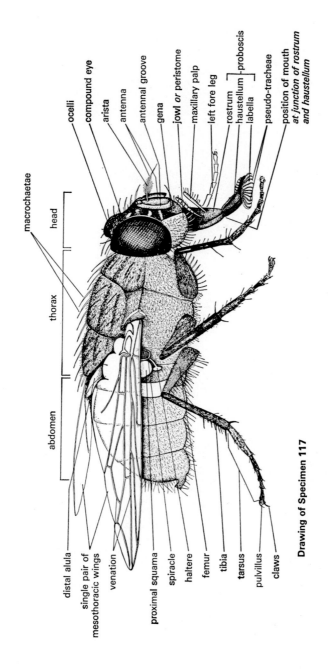

Drawing of Specimen 117

macrochaetae

head

thorax

abdomen

ocelli

compound eye

arista

antenna

antennal groove

gena

jowl or peristome

maxillary palp

left fore leg

rostrum

haustellum ⎤ proboscis
labella ⎦

pseudo-tracheae

position of mouth
*at junction of rostrum
and haustellum*

distal alula

single pair of
mesothoracic wings

venation

proximal squama

spiracle

haltere

femur

tibia

tarsus

pulvillus

claws

118. *Spilopsyllus*, E. Mag. ×30

PARASITIC INSECTS

Four adult insects have been selected to illustrate specialisation for parasitism in the class.

The Siphonaptera (fleas) are flattened laterally, whereas the keds are flattened dorso-ventrally. The mouth-parts are broad-bladed, incorporating an anti-coagulant pump and pharyngeal sucking apparatus. The insects are modified to jump large distances.

119. *Cimex*, E. Mag. ×16

The Hemiptera (the bugs) include many plant feeders as well as true parasites. The bed bug *Cimex* has typical bug mouthparts of the rostrum type, held between the bases of the legs when at rest. The bed bug is flattened dorso-ventrally.

88

The Diptera (flies) are usually very mobile, but the sheep ked *Melophagus* has become completely wingless, and has modified claws for clinging to the host. Retractable sucking mouthparts are present in both sexes.

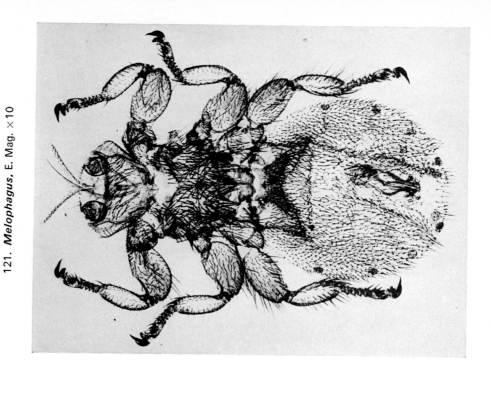

121. *Melophagus*, E. Mag. ×10

The human body louse (*Pediculus humanus corporis*) belongs in the Anoplura, and has highly modified mouthparts, retracted into the head when not in use. The animal is a serious pest, since it carries typhus and relapsing fever.

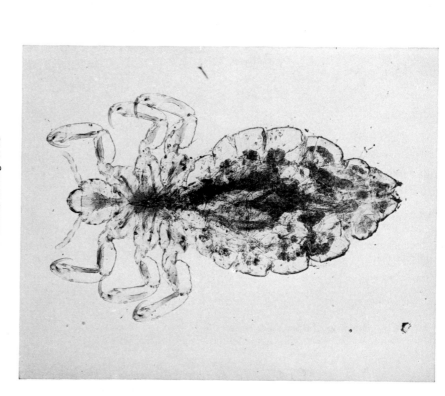

120. *Pediculus*, E. Mag. ×13

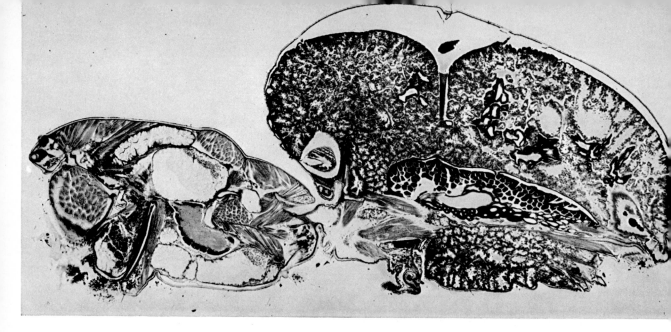

122. *Aranea*, LS. Mag. ×14

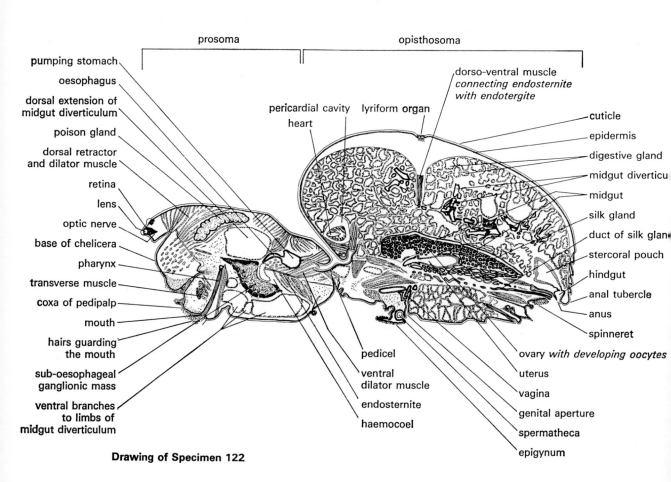

prosoma   opisthosoma

pumping stomach

oesophagus

dorsal extension of
midgut diverticulum

poison gland

dorsal retractor
and dilator muscle

retina

lens

optic nerve

base of chelicera

pharynx

transverse muscle

coxa of pedipalp

mouth

hairs guarding
the mouth

sub-oesophageal
ganglionic mass

ventral branches
to limbs of
midgut diverticulum

pericardial cavity
heart

lyriform organ

dorso-ventral muscle
*connecting endosternite
with endotergite*

cuticle

epidermis

digestive gland

midgut diverticu

midgut

silk gland

duct of silk glan

stercoral pouch

hindgut

anal tubercle

anus

spinneret

ovary *with developing oocytes*

uterus

vagina

genital aperture

spermatheca

epigynum

pedicel

ventral
dilator muscle

endosternite

haemocoel

Drawing of Specimen 122

91

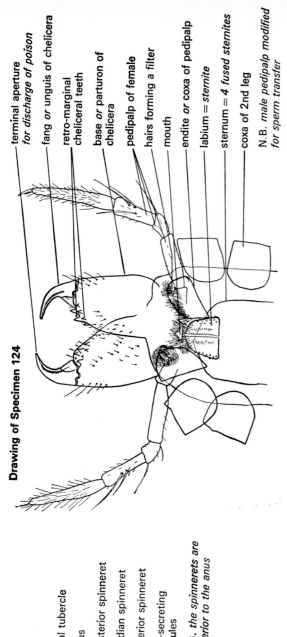

Drawing of Specimen 124

- terminal aperture *for discharge of poison*
- fang *or* unguis of chelicera
- retro-marginal cheliceral teeth
- base *or* parturon of chelicera
- pedipalp of female
- hairs forming a filter
- mouth
- endite *or* coxa of pedipalp
- labium = *sternite*
- sternum = *4 fused sternites*
- coxa of 2nd leg

N.B. *male pedipalp modified for sperm transfer*

- anal tubercle
- anus
- posterior spinneret
- median spinneret
- anterior spinneret
- silk-secreting tubules

N.B. *the spinnerets are anterior to the anus*

Drawing of Specimen 123

124. *Aranea*, prosoma E. Mag. × 25

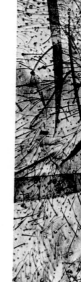

123. *Aranea*, spinnerettes, E. Mag. × 55

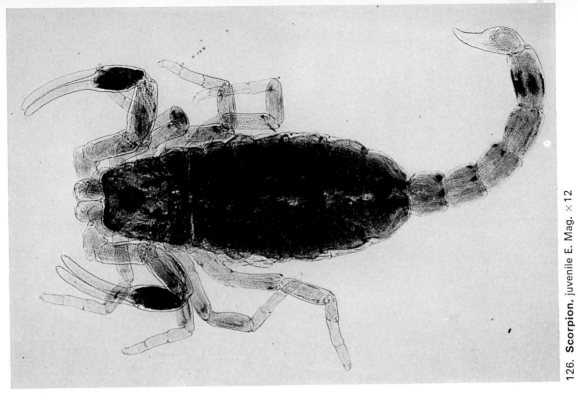

126. **Scorpion**, juvenile E. Mag. ×12

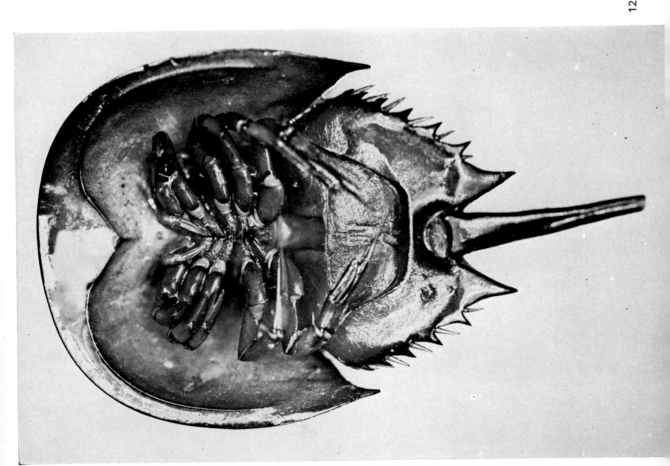

125. *Xiphosura*, ventral surface E. Mag. ×3

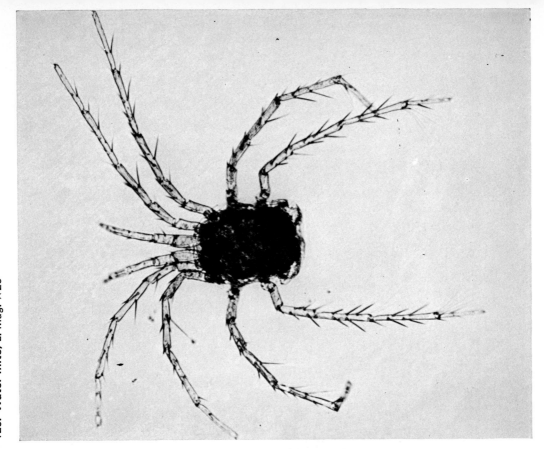

128. Water mite, E. Mag. ×25

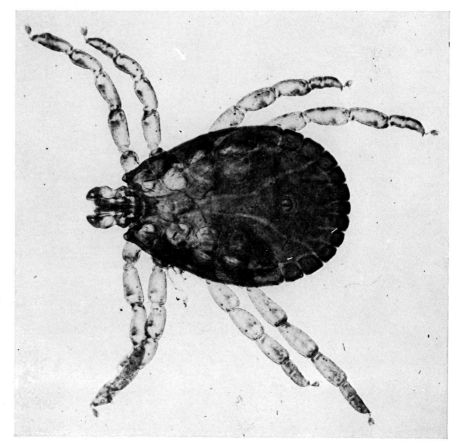

127. *Dermacentor*, E. Mag. ×8

93

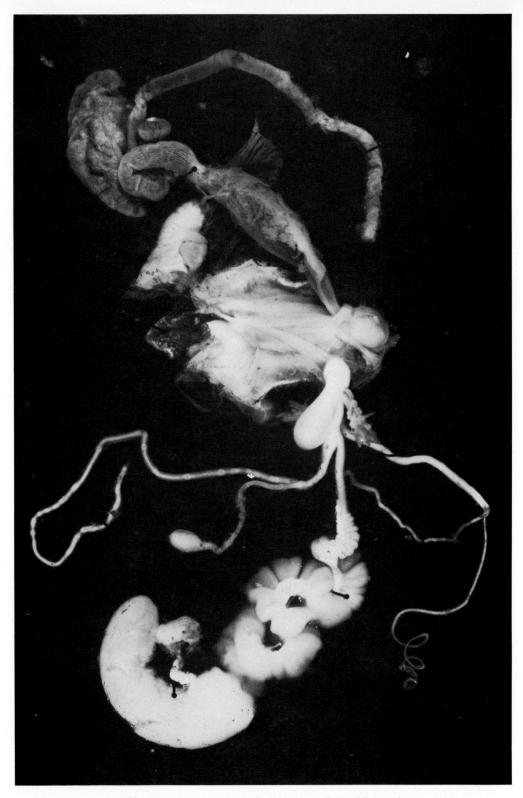

129. *Helix,* general dissection, fresh specimen. Mag. ×2

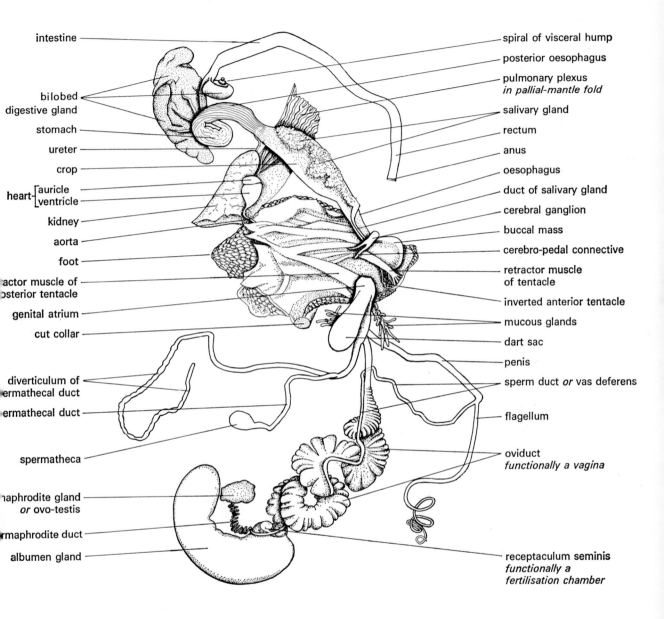

intestine — spiral of visceral hump

posterior oesophagus

pulmonary plexus
in pallial-mantle fold

bilobed
digestive gland

salivary gland

stomach — rectum

ureter — anus

crop — oesophagus

heart [auricle
       ventricle]

duct of salivary gland

cerebral ganglion

kidney — buccal mass

aorta — cerebro-pedal connective

foot — retractor muscle
       of tentacle

actor muscle of
osterior tentacle

inverted anterior tentacle

genital atrium — mucous glands

cut collar — dart sac

penis

diverticulum of
ermathecal duct

sperm duct *or* vas deferens

ermathecal duct — flagellum

spermatheca

oviduct
functionally a vagina

naphrodite gland
or ovo-testis

rmaphrodite duct

albumen gland — receptaculum **seminis**
*functionally a
fertilisation chamber*

Drawing of Specimen 129

95

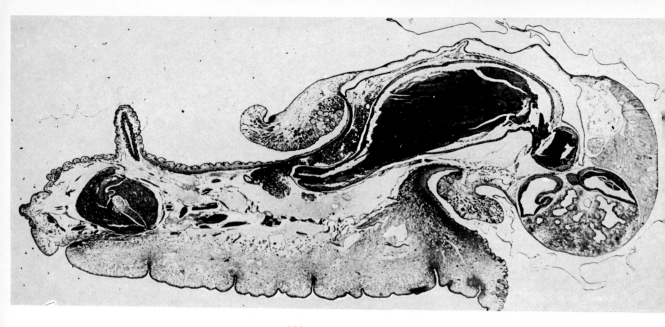

130. *Limnaea,* LS. Mag. ×8

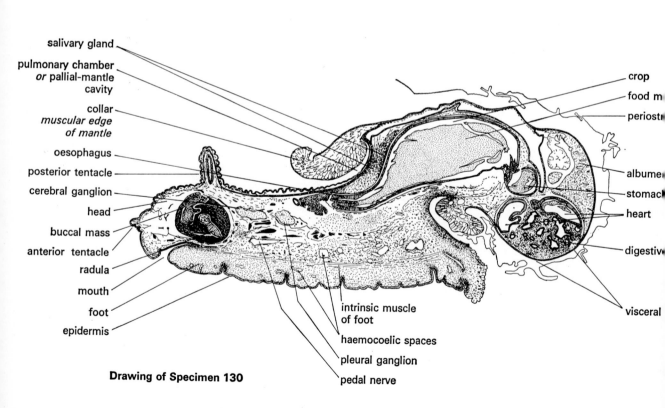

salivary gland

pulmonary chamber
or pallial-mantle
cavity

collar
*muscular edge
of mantle*

oesophagus

posterior tentacle

cerebral ganglion

head

buccal mass

anterior tentacle

radula

mouth

foot

epidermis

crop

food m

periost

albume

stomac

heart

digestive

visceral

intrinsic muscle
of foot

haemocoelic spaces

pleural ganglion

pedal nerve

Drawing of Specimen 130

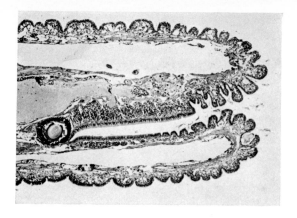

131. *Helix*, tentacle and eye, LS. Mag. ×115

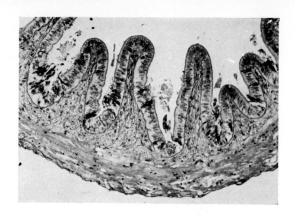

132. *Helix*, intestine, TS. Mag. ×125

The eye is at the tip of a retractable tentacle, and the retractor muscle can be seen applied to the end of the invagination. The tentacle is extended by the tissue which resembles mammalian erectile tissue in appearance and function. The eye is simple, with a transparent epidermal covering, large lens, retina, and fibres forming an optic nerve.

The intestinal epithelium consists of mucus cells and ciliated columnar cells (the cilia visible in prepared slides if phase contrast illumination is used). Inner longitudinal and outer circular fibres are present.

HISTOLOGY OF *HELIX*

The crop is a thin-walled dilation of the oesophagus, lined with columnar epithelium. Cilia are present intermittently, with goblet cells singly or in clusters.

133. *Helix*, crop and salivary gland, TS. Mag. ×120

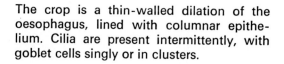

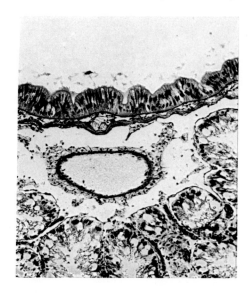

The 'liver' (better called the digestive gland), is bilobed. Two kinds of cell are present. Digestive cells are columnar, with secretory granules distally. Calciferous cells are cuboidal, with granules of calcium phosphate. The ducts are heavily ciliated.

134. *Helix*, 'liver' and bile duct TS. Mag. ×120

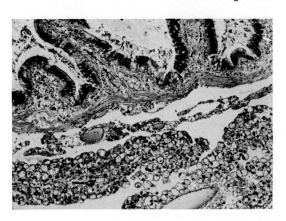

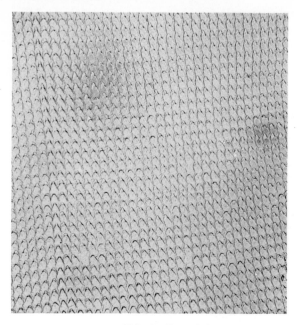

135. *Helix,* radula E. Mag. ×120

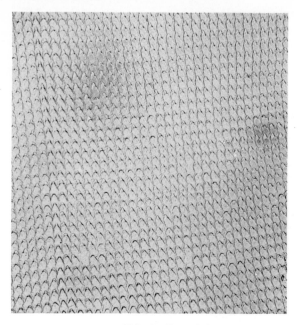

136. *Buccinum,* radula E. Mag. ×55

137. *Trochus,* radula E ,reflected light. Mag. ×40

138. *Anodonta,* general dissection, fresh specimen. Mag. ×1

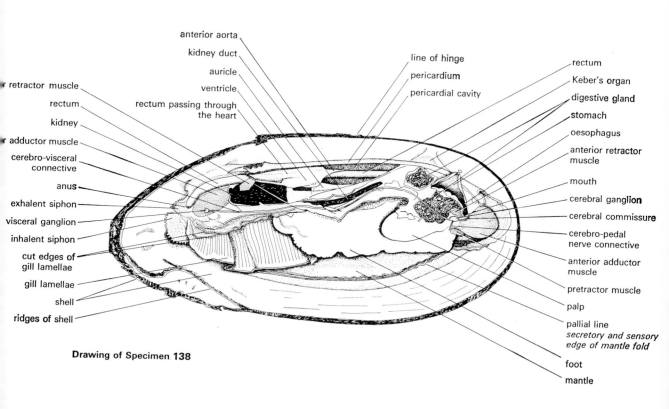

anterior aorta
kidney duct
auricle
ventricle
rectum passing through
the heart

line of hinge
pericardium
pericardial cavity

rectum
Keber's organ
digestive gland
stomach
oesophagus
anterior retractor
muscle
mouth
cerebral ganglion
cerebral commissure
cerebro-pedal
nerve connective
anterior adductor
muscle
pretractor muscle
palp
pallial line
*secretory and sensory
edge of mantle fold*
foot
mantle

retractor muscle
rectum
kidney
adductor muscle
cerebro-visceral
connective
anus
exhalent siphon
visceral ganglion
inhalent siphon
cut edges of
gill lamellae
gill lamellae
shell
ridges of shell

Drawing of Specimen 138

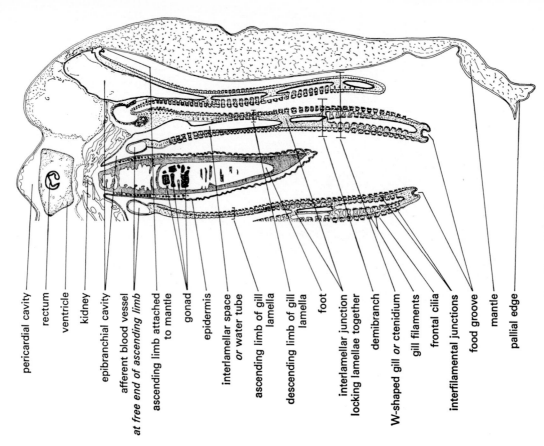

pericardial cavity
rectum
ventricle
kidney
epibranchial cavity
afferent blood vessel
at free end of ascending limb
ascending limb attached
to mantle
gonad
epidermis
interlamellar space
or water tube
ascending limb of gill
lamella
descending limb of gill
lamella
foot
interlamellar junction
locking lamellae together
demibranch
W-shaped gill *or ctenidium*
gill filaments
frontal cilia
interfilamental junctions
food groove
mantle
pallial edge

Drawing of Specimen 139

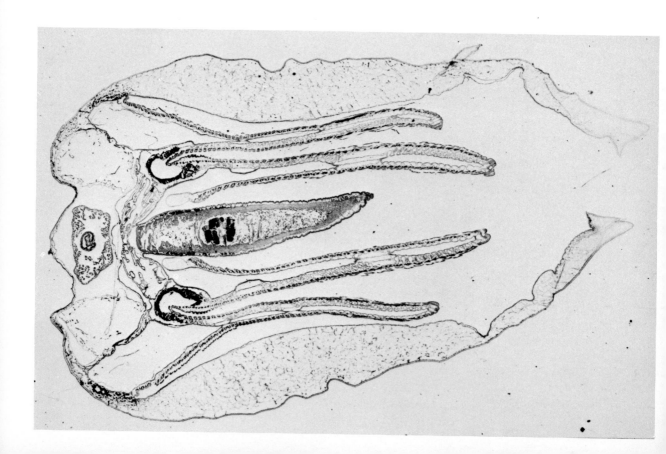

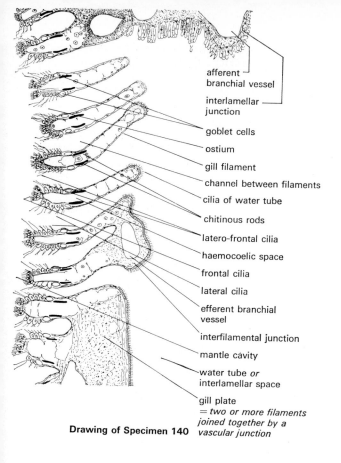

afferent branchial vessel

interlamellar junction

goblet cells

ostium

gill filament

channel between filaments

cilia of water tube

chitinous rods

latero-frontal cilia

haemocoelic space

frontal cilia

lateral cilia

efferent branchial vessel

interfilamental junction

mantle cavity

water tube *or* interlamellar space

gill plate
= *two or more filaments joined together by a vascular junction*

Drawing of Specimen 140

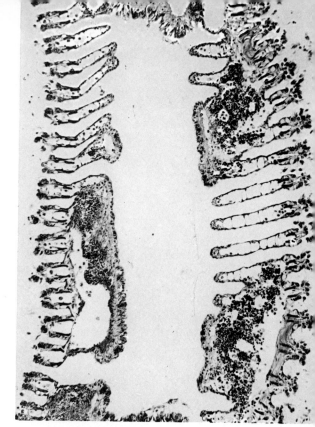

140. ***Anodonta***, ctenidium TS. Mag. ×50

141. ***Anodonta***, glochidium larva E. Mag. ×125

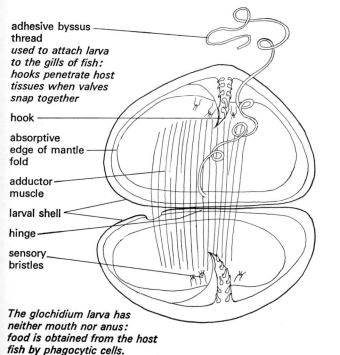

adhesive byssus thread
used to attach larva to the gills of fish: hooks penetrate host tissues when valves snap together

hook

absorptive edge of mantle fold

adductor muscle

larval shell

hinge

sensory bristles

The glochidium larva has neither mouth nor anus: food is obtained from the host fish by phagocytic cells.

Drawing of Specimen 141

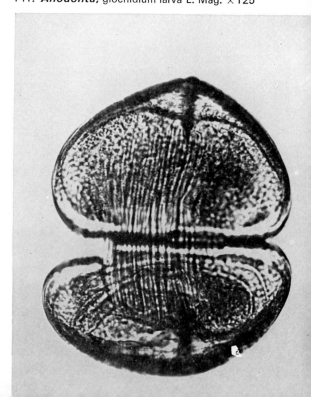

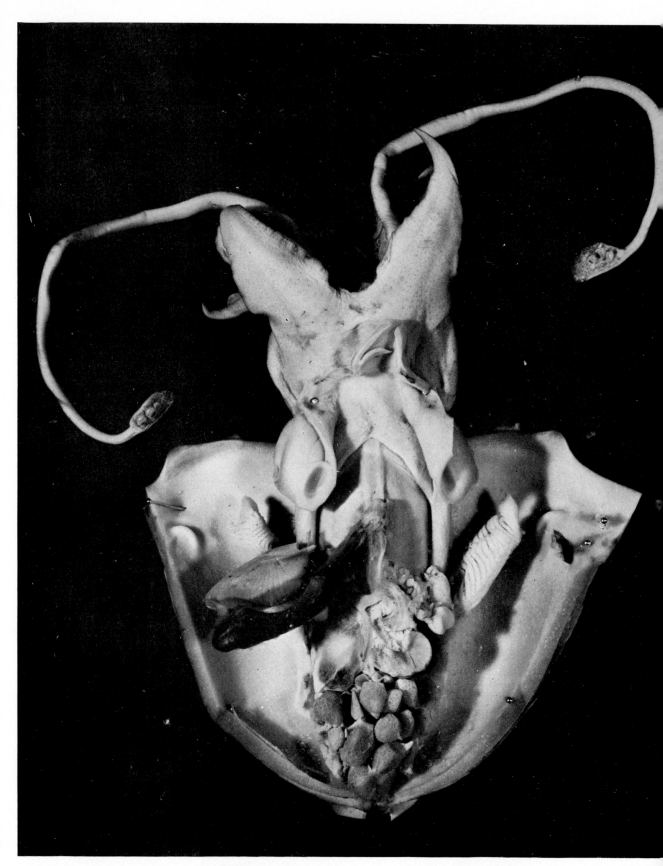

142. *Sepia,* general dissection, preserved specimen. Mag. ×1.5

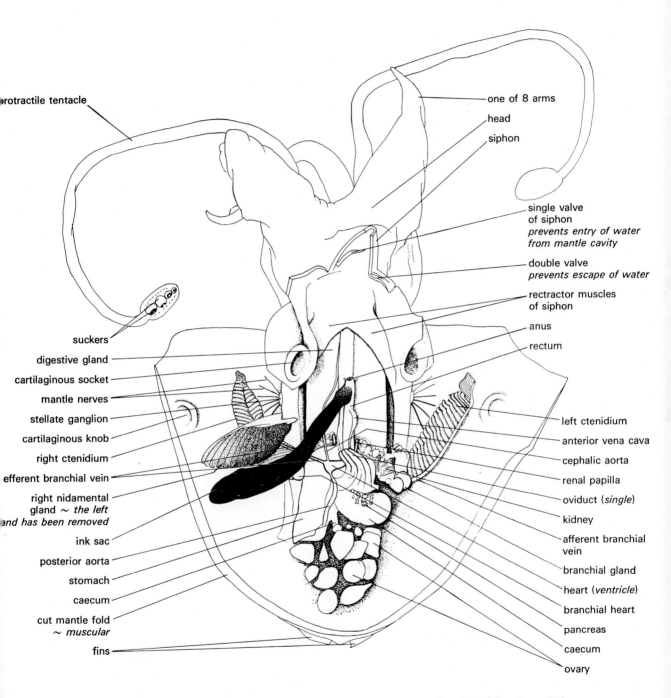

protractile tentacle

one of 8 arms

head

siphon

single valve
of siphon
*prevents entry of water
from mantle cavity*

double valve
prevents escape of water

rectractor muscles
of siphon

anus

rectum

suckers

digestive gland

cartilaginous socket

mantle nerves

stellate ganglion

cartilaginous knob

right ctenidium

efferent branchial vein

right nidamental
gland ~ *the left
and has been removed*

ink sac

posterior aorta

stomach

caecum

cut mantle fold
~ *muscular*

fins

left ctenidium

anterior vena cava

cephalic aorta

renal papilla

oviduct (*single*)

kidney

afferent branchial
vein

branchial gland

heart (*ventricle*)

branchial heart

pancreas

caecum

ovary

Drawing of Specimen 142

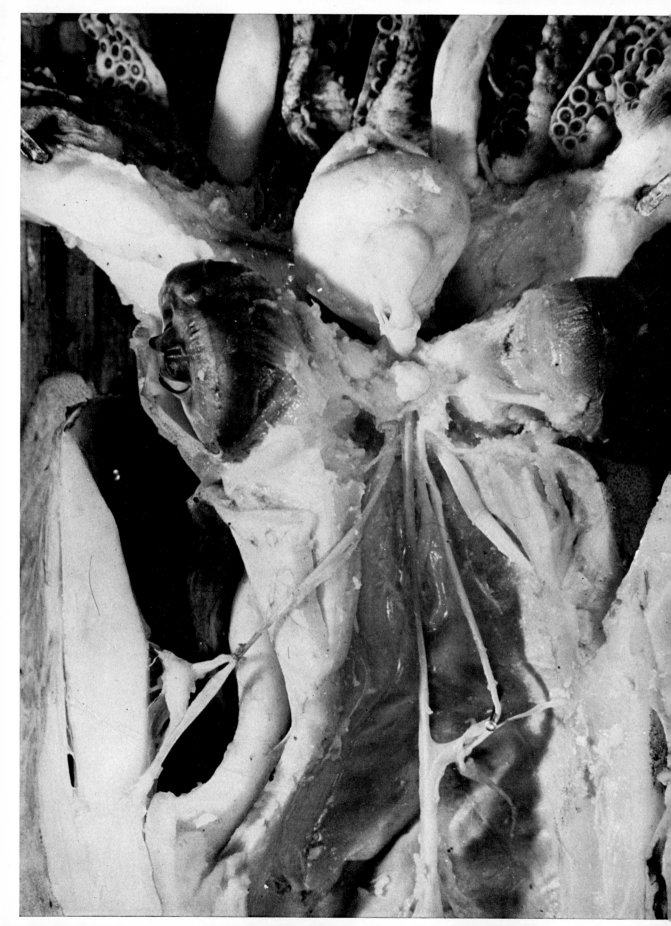

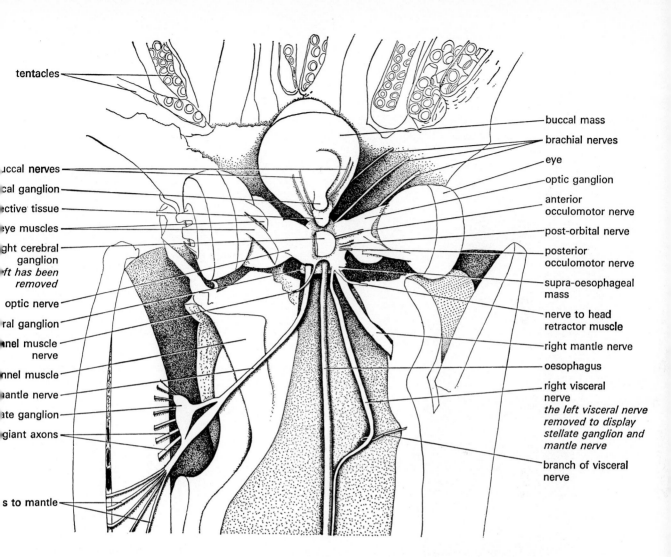

tentacles

buccal nerves
ccal ganglion
ective tissue
eye muscles
ght cerebral
ganglion
ft has been
removed
optic nerve
ral ganglion
nnel muscle
nerve
nnel muscle
antle nerve
ate ganglion
giant axons

s to mantle

buccal mass
brachial nerves
eye
optic ganglion
anterior
occulomotor nerve
post-orbital nerve
posterior
occulomotor nerve
supra-oesophageal
mass
nerve to head
retractor muscle
right mantle nerve
oesophagus
right visceral
nerve
*the left visceral nerve
removed to display
stellate ganglion and
mantle nerve*
branch of visceral
nerve

Drawing of Specimen 143

*a dorsal approach was used on the right side of this
dissection and a lateral approach on the left side.*

3. *Sepia*, dissection of **nervous** system, preserved specimen. Mag. ×2

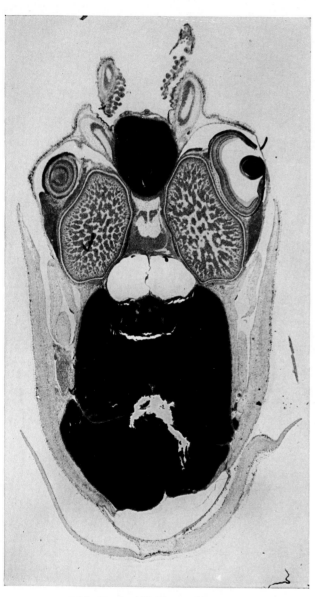

144. *Sepia*, HS. Mag. ×10

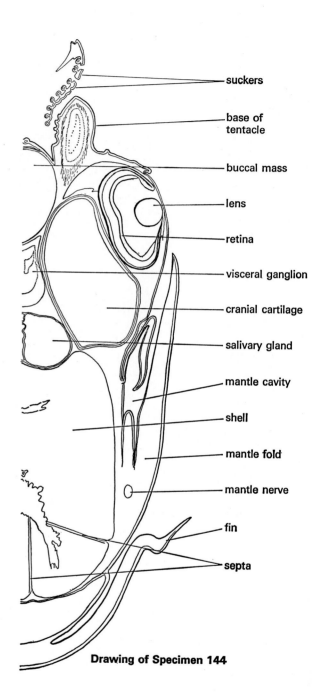

suckers

base of
tentacle

buccal mass

lens

retina

visceral ganglion

cranial cartilage

salivary gland

mantle cavity

shell

mantle fold

mantle nerve

fin

septa

Drawing of Specimen 144

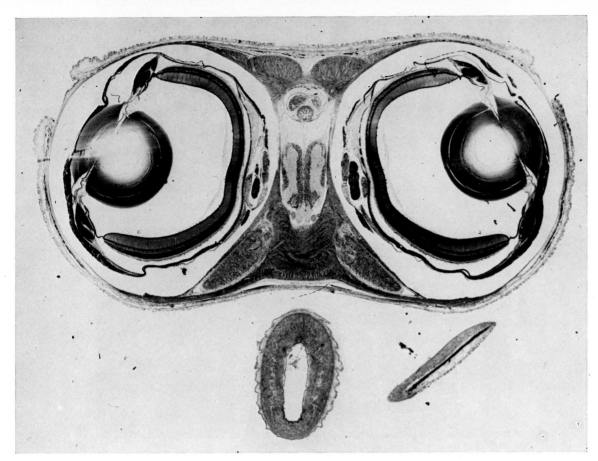

145. *Sepiolia*, head TS. Mag. ×10

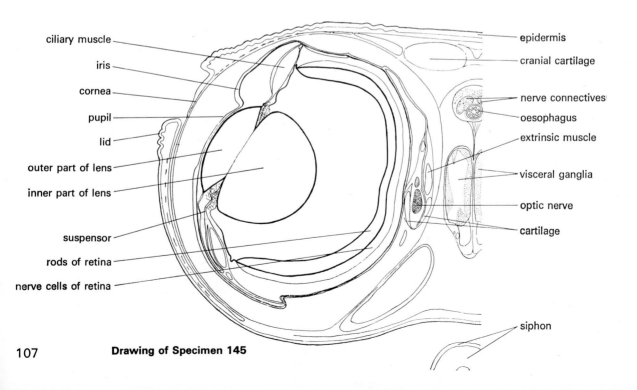

ciliary muscle

iris

cornea

pupil

lid

outer part of lens

inner part of lens

suspensor

rods of retina

nerve cells of retina

epidermis

cranial cartilage

nerve connectives

oesophagus

extrinsic muscle

visceral ganglia

optic nerve

cartilage

siphon

Drawing of Specimen 145

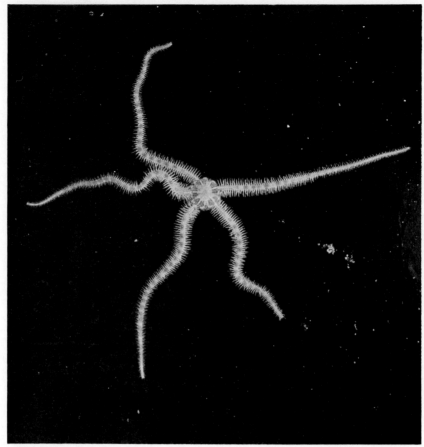

146. **Brittle star,** living. Mag. ×1

147. **Sea cucumber,** living. Mag. ×0.5

148. **Feather star,** living. Mag. ×0.7

149. *Asterias,* general dissection fresh specimen. Mag. ×1

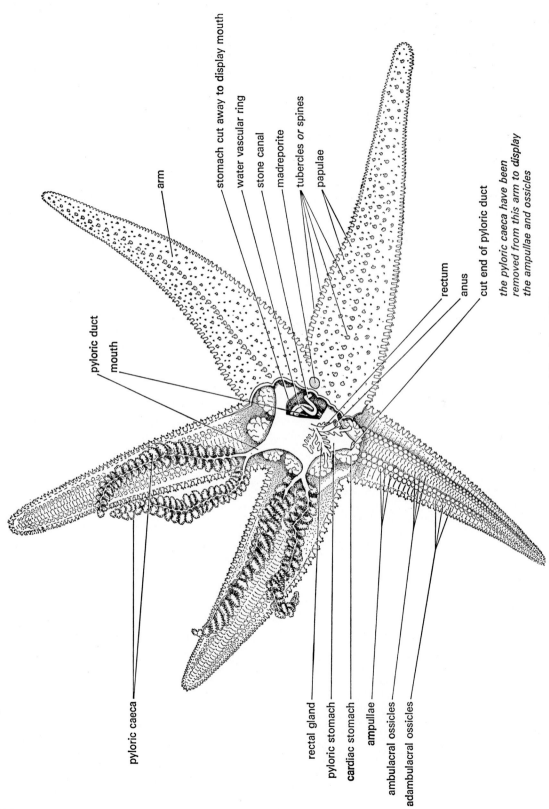

arm

stomach cut away to display mouth

water vascular ring

stone canal

madreporite

tubercles *or* spines

papulae

rectum

anus

cut end of pyloric duct

the pyloric caeca have been
removed from this arm to display
the ampullae and ossicles

pyloric duct

mouth

pyloric caeca

rectal gland

pyloric stomach

cardiac stomach

ampullae

ambulacral ossicles

adambulacral ossicles

Drawing of Specimen 149

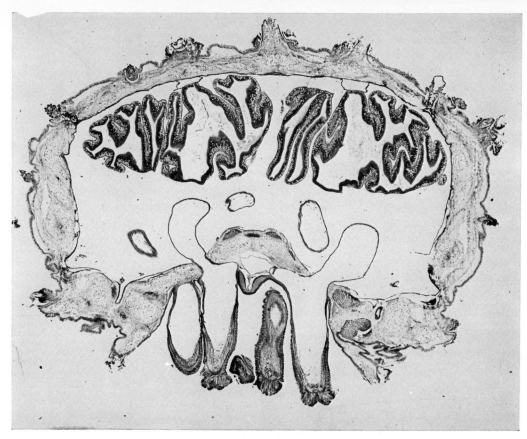

150. *Asterias*, arm TS. Mag. ×15

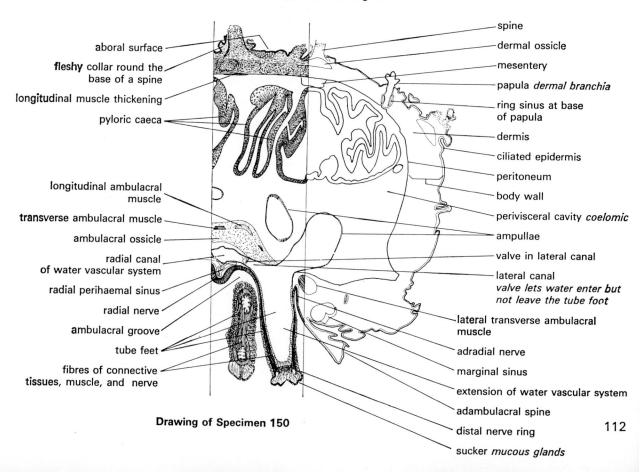

aboral surface

fleshy collar round the base of a spine

longitudinal muscle thickening

pyloric caeca

longitudinal ambulacral muscle

transverse ambulacral muscle

ambulacral ossicle

radial canal of water vascular system

radial perihaemal sinus

radial nerve

ambulacral groove

tube feet

fibres of connective tissues, muscle, and nerve

spine

dermal ossicle

mesentery

papula *dermal branchia*

ring sinus at base of papula

dermis

ciliated epidermis

peritoneum

body wall

perivisceral cavity *coelomic*

ampullae

valve in lateral canal

lateral canal
valve lets water enter but not leave the tube foot

lateral transverse ambulacral muscle

adradial nerve

marginal sinus

extension of water vascular system

adambulacral spine

distal nerve ring

sucker *mucous glands*

Drawing of Specimen 150

112

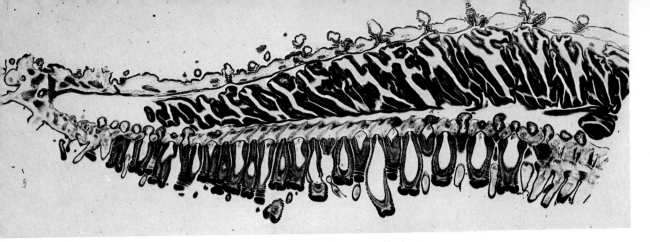

151. *Asterias*, arm LS. Mag. ×12

Drawing of Specimen 151

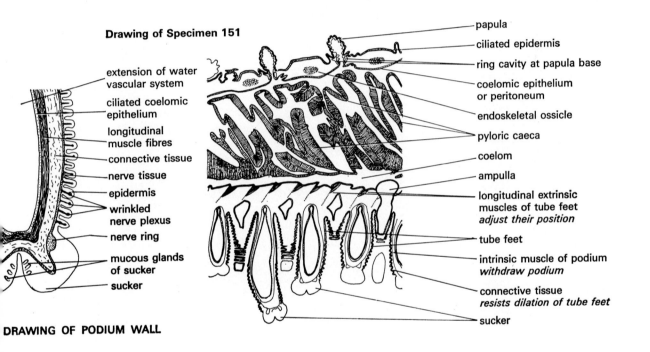

extension of water vascular system

ciliated coelomic epithelium

longitudinal muscle fibres

connective tissue

nerve tissue

epidermis

wrinkled nerve plexus

nerve ring

mucous glands of sucker

sucker

DRAWING OF PODIUM WALL

papula

ciliated epidermis

ring cavity at papula base

coelomic epithelium or peritoneum

endoskeletal ossicle

pyloric caeca

coelom

ampulla

longitudinal extrinsic muscles of tube feet *adjust their position*

tube feet

intrinsic muscle of podium *withdraw podium*

connective tissue *resists dilation of tube feet*

sucker

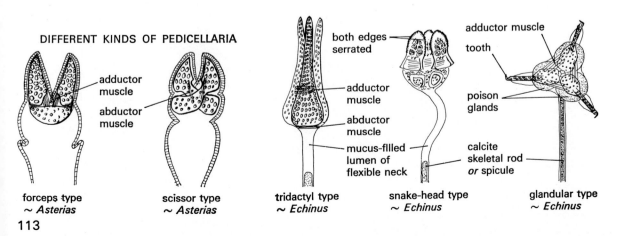

DIFFERENT KINDS OF PEDICELLARIA

adductor muscle

abductor muscle

forceps type ~ *Asterias*

scissor type ~ *Asterias*

both edges serrated

adductor muscle

abductor muscle

mucus-filled lumen of flexible neck

tridactyl type ~ *Echinus*

adductor muscle

tooth

poison glands

calcite skeletal rod *or* spicule

snake-head type ~ *Echinus*

glandular type ~ *Echinus*

113

152. *Echinus,* general dissection, fresh specimen. Mag. ×1.2

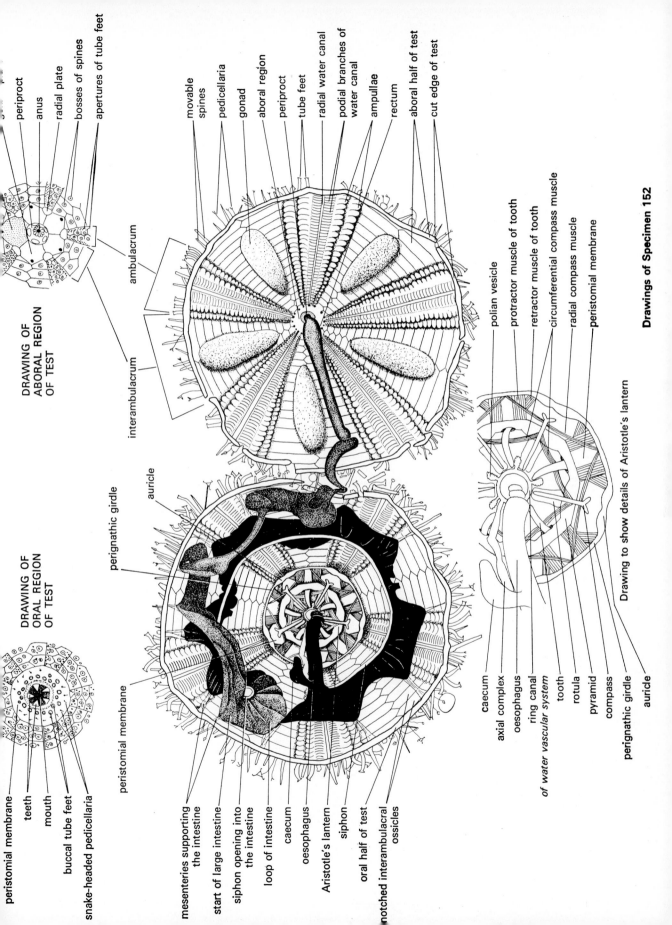

DRAWING OF ABORAL REGION OF TEST

periproct
anus
radial plate
bosses of spines
apertures of tube feet

movable spines
pedicellaria
gonad
aboral region
periproct
tube feet
radial water canal
podial branches of water canal
ampullae
rectum
aboral half of test
cut edge of test

ambulacrum
interambulacrum

DRAWING OF ORAL REGION OF TEST

peristomial membrane
teeth
mouth
buccal tube feet
snake-headed pedicellaria

peristomial membrane

auricle
perignathic girdle

peristomial membrane

mesenteries supporting the intestine
start of large intestine
siphon opening into the intestine
loop of intestine
caecum
oesophagus
Aristotle's lantern
siphon
oral half of test
notched interambulacral ossicles

polian vesicle
protractor muscle of tooth
retractor muscle of tooth
circumferential compass muscle
radial compass muscle
peristomial membrane

caecum
axial complex
oesophagus
ring canal
of water vascular system
tooth
rotula
pyramid
compass
perignathic girdle
auricle

Drawing to show details of Aristotle's lantern

Drawings of Specimen 152

153. *Echinus*, living, laying eggs. Mag. ×1

154. **Aristotle's lantern,** E, in situ. Mag. ×1

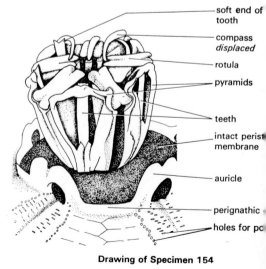

soft end of tooth

compass *displaced*

rotula

pyramids

teeth

intact perist
membrane

auricle

perignathic

holes for po

Drawing of Specimen 154

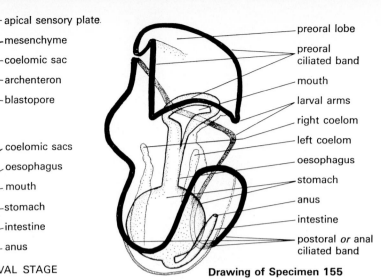

ASTRULA

- apical sensory plate
- mesenchyme
- coelomic sac
- archenteron
- blastopore

EE—LIVING LARVAL STAGE

- coelomic sacs
- oesophagus
- mouth
- stomach
- intestine
- anus

- preoral lobe
- preoral ciliated band
- mouth
- larval arms
- right coelom
- left coelom
- oesophagus
- stomach
- anus
- intestine
- postoral *or* anal ciliated band

Drawing of Specimen 155

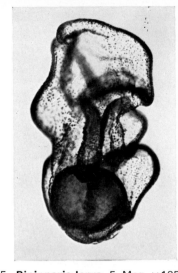

155. **Bipinnaria larva,** E. Mag. ×135

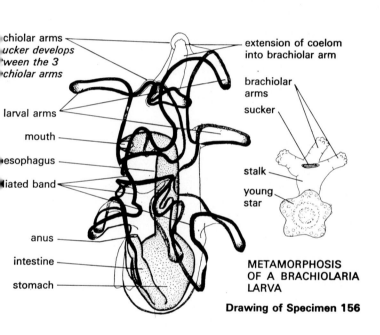

- chiolar arms
- ucker develops 'ween the 3 'chiolar arms
- larval arms
- mouth
- esophagus
- liated band
- anus
- intestine
- stomach

- extension of coelom into brachiolar arm
- brachiolar arms
- sucker
- stalk
- young star

METAMORPHOSIS OF A BRACHIOLARIA LARVA

Drawing of Specimen 156

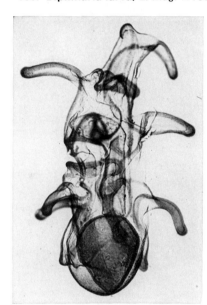

156. **Brachiolaria larva,** E. Mag. ×65

157. **Pluteus larva,** E. Mag. ×105

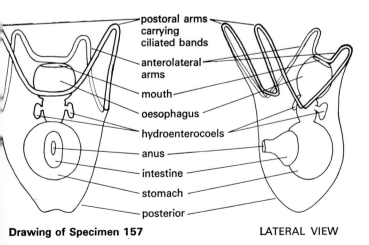

- postoral arms carrying ciliated bands
- anterolateral arms
- mouth
- oesophagus
- hydroenterocoels
- anus
- intestine
- stomach
- posterior

Drawing of Specimen 157

LATERAL VIEW

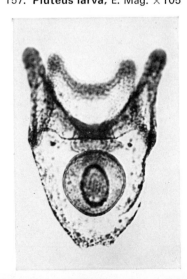

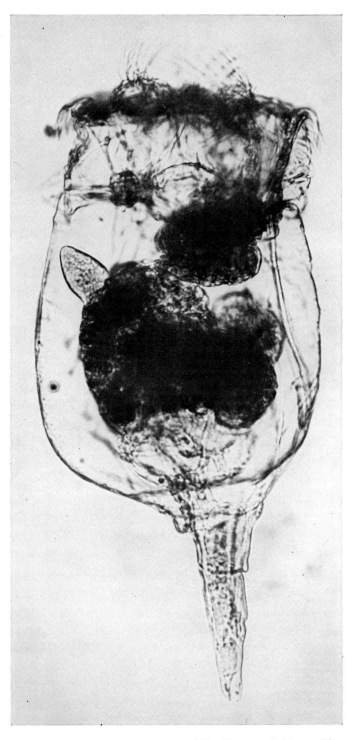

158. *Notops*, E. Mag. ×90

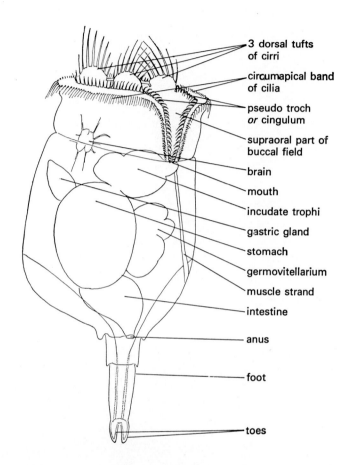

3 dorsal tufts
of cirri

circumapical band
of cilia

pseudo troch
or cingulum

supraoral part of
buccal field

brain

mouth

incudate trophi

gastric gland

stomach

germovitellarium

muscle strand

intestine

anus

foot

toes

Drawing of Specimen 158

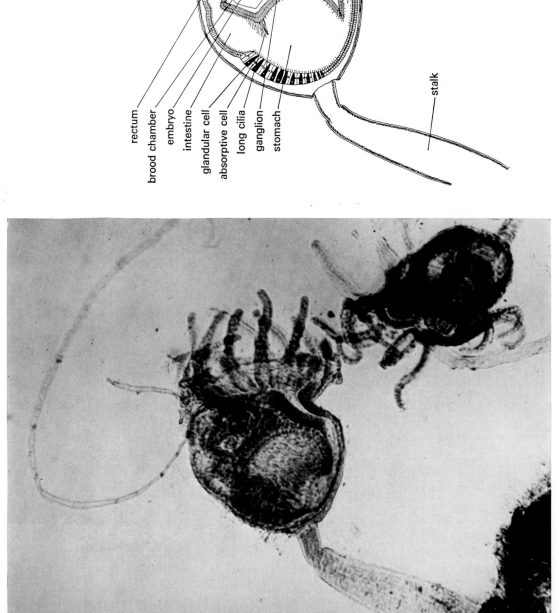

calyx

margin of intertentacular membrane

tentacular crown

large mesenchyme cells

pseudocoel

anal cone

anus

gonopore

gonoduct

mouth

tentacle

buccal funnel

oesophagus

cuticle

epidermis

Drawing of Specimen 159

rectum

brood chamber

embryo

intestine

glandular cell

absorptive cell

long cilia

ganglion

stomach

stalk

159. *Pedicellina*, E. Mag. ×85

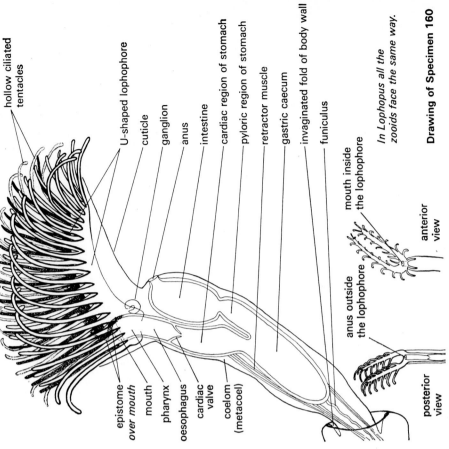

hollow ciliated
tentacles

U-shaped lophophore
cuticle
ganglion
anus
intestine
cardiac region of stomach
pyloric region of stomach
retractor muscle
gastric caecum
invaginated fold of body wall
funiculus

mouth inside
the lophophore

anus outside
the lophophore

*In Lophopus all the
zooids face the same way.*

Drawing of Specimen 160

anterior
view

posterior
view

epistome
over mouth
mouth
pharynx
oesophagus
cardiac
valve
coelom
(metacoel)

160. *Lophopus*, E. Mag. × 45

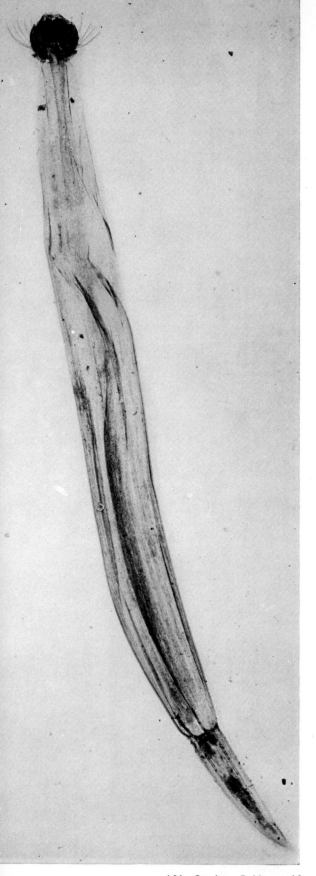

161. *Sagitta,* E. Mag. ×10

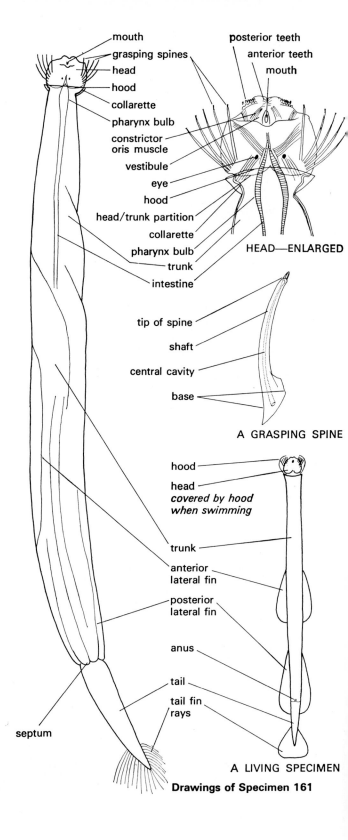

mouth
grasping spines
head
hood
collarette
pharynx bulb
constrictor
oris muscle
vestibule
eye
hood
head/trunk partition
collarette
pharynx bulb
trunk
intestine

posterior teeth
anterior teeth
mouth

HEAD—ENLARGED

tip of spine
shaft
central cavity
base

A GRASPING SPINE

hood
head
*covered by hood
when swimming*

trunk

anterior
lateral fin

posterior
lateral fin

anus

tail

tail fin
rays

septum

A LIVING SPECIMEN

Drawings of Specimen 161

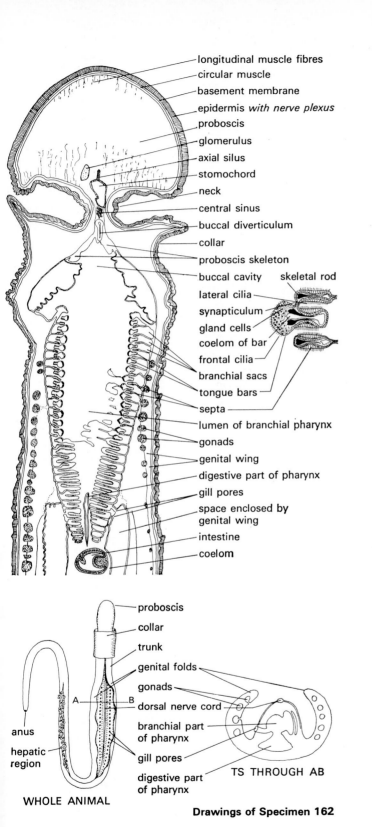

longitudinal muscle fibres
circular muscle
basement membrane
epidermis *with nerve plexus*
proboscis
glomerulus
axial silus
stomochord
neck
central sinus
buccal diverticulum
collar
proboscis skeleton
buccal cavity
skeletal rod
lateral cilia
synapticulum
gland cells
coelom of bar
frontal cilia
branchial sacs
tongue bars
septa
lumen of branchial pharynx
gonads
genital wing
digestive part of pharynx
gill pores
space enclosed by genital wing
intestine
coelom

proboscis
collar
trunk
genital folds
gonads
dorsal nerve cord
branchial part of pharynx
gill pores
digestive part of pharynx

anus
hepatic region

A   B

TS THROUGH AB

WHOLE ANIMAL

Drawings of Specimen 162

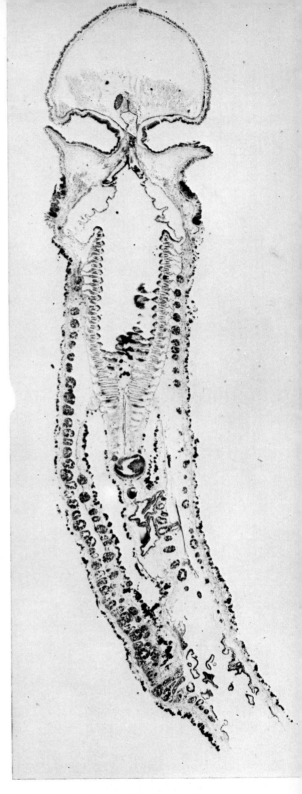

162. *Dolichoglossus*, HS. Mag. ×20

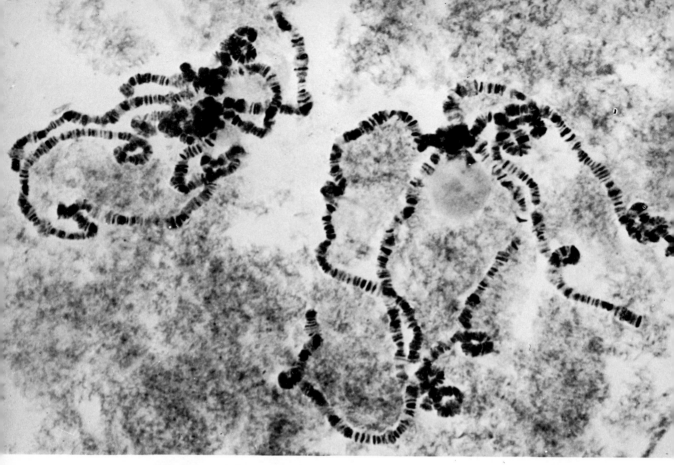

163. **Chromosomes from *Drosophila* salivary gland squash. Mag.** ×225

164. (a) **Polar body—*Asterias* egg. Mag.** ×250

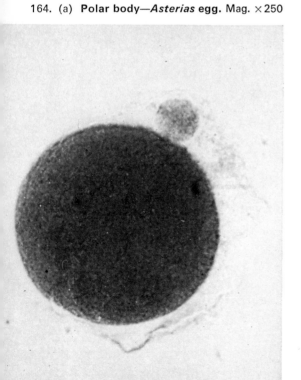

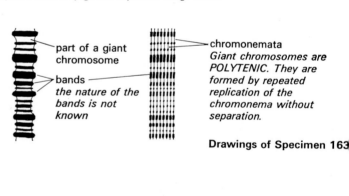

part of a giant chromosome

bands
the nature of the bands is not known

chromonemata
Giant chromosomes are POLYTENIC. They are formed by repeated replication of the chromonema without separation.

Drawings of Specimen 163

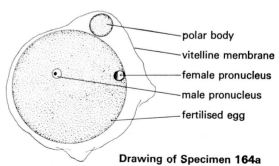

polar body

vitelline membrane

female pronucleus

male pronucleus

fertilised egg

Drawing of Specimen 164a

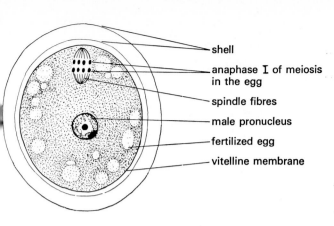

shell

anaphase I of meiosis
in the egg

spindle fibres

male pronucleus

fertilized egg

vitelline membrane

Drawing of Specimen 164b

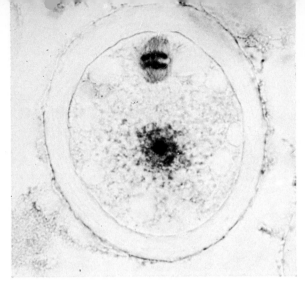

(b) **Polar body—*Ascaris* egg,** anaphase of first
maturation division.

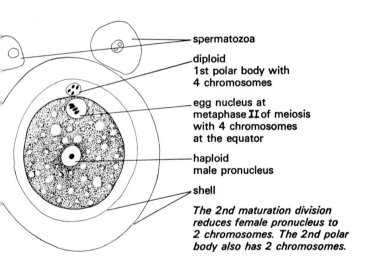

spermatozoa

diploid
1st polar body with
4 chromosomes

egg nucleus at
metaphase II of meiosis
with 4 chromosomes
at the equator

haploid
male pronucleus

shell

The 2nd maturation division
reduces female pronucleus to
2 chromosomes. The 2nd polar
body also has 2 chromosomes.

Drawing of Specimen 164c

Both Mag. ×575

(c) **Polar body—*Ascaris* egg,** metaphase of second
maturation division.

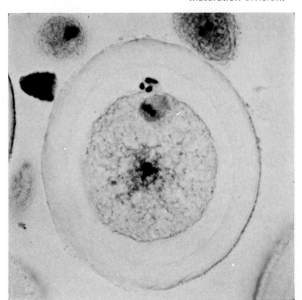

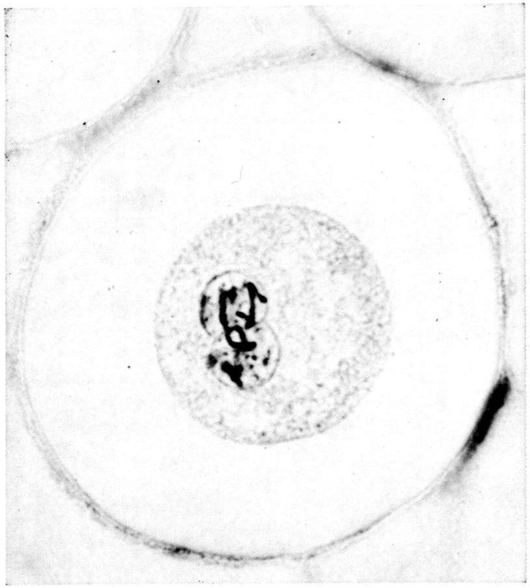

(a) Prophase; male and female pronuclei

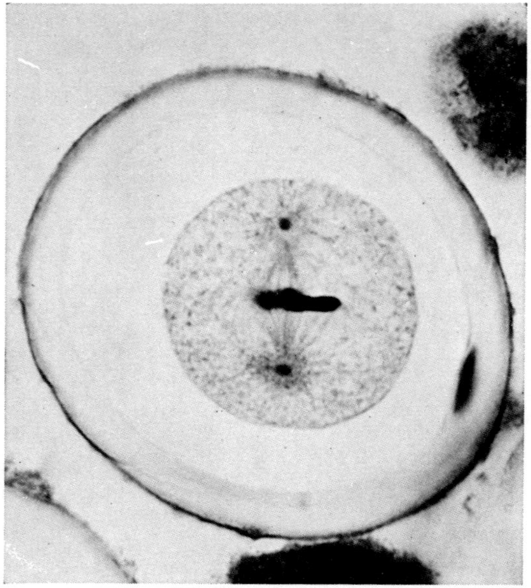

(b) Metaphase, spindle cut longitudinally

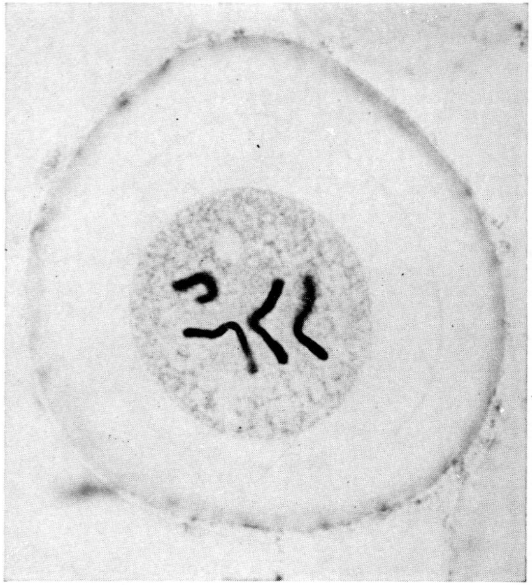

(c) Metaphase, spindle cut in equatorial plane

(d) Anaphase

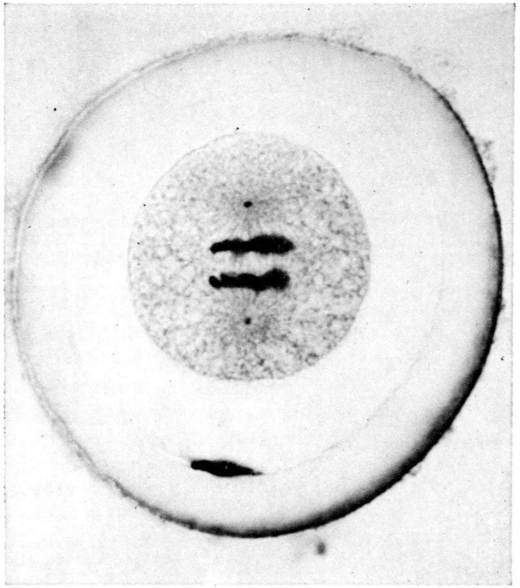

(e) Telophase

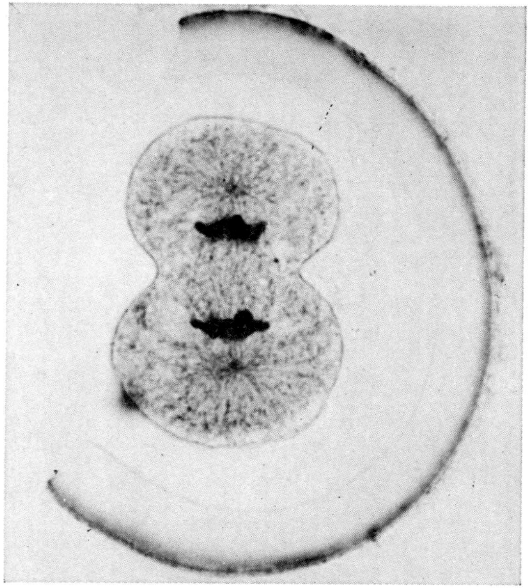

(f) First cleavage furrow of zygote

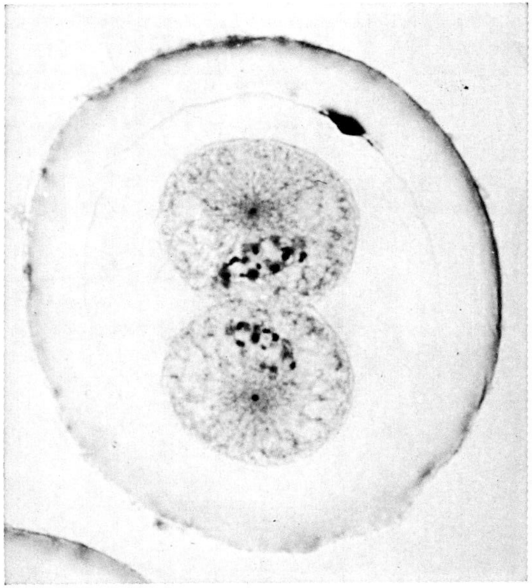

165. **Mitosis stages from developing *Ascaris* zygotes. All Mag. ×580**

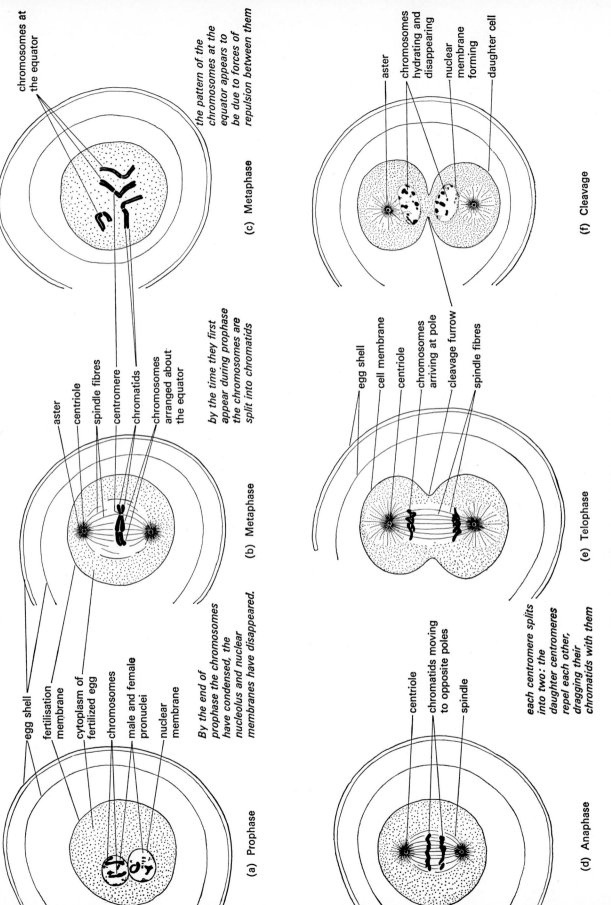

(a) Prophase

egg shell
fertilisation membrane
cytoplasm of fertilized egg
chromosomes
male and female pronuclei
nuclear membrane

By the end of prophase the chromosomes have condensed, the nucleolus and nuclear membranes have disappeared.

(b) Metaphase

aster
centriole
spindle fibres
centromere
chromatids
chromosomes arranged about the equator

by the time they first appear during prophase the chromosomes are split into chromatids

(c) Metaphase

chromosomes at the equator

the pattern of the chromosomes at the equator appears to be due to forces of repulsion between them

(d) Anaphase

centriole
chromatids moving to opposite poles
spindle

each centromere splits into two: the daughter centromeres repel each other, dragging their chromatids with them

(e) Telophase

egg shell
cell membrane
centriole
chromosomes arriving at pole
cleavage furrow
spindle fibres

(f) Cleavage

aster
chromosomes hydrating and disappearing
nuclear membrane forming
daughter cell

Drawings of Specimens 165a, b, c, d, e, f

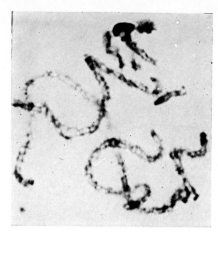

(a) Prophase I, leptonema

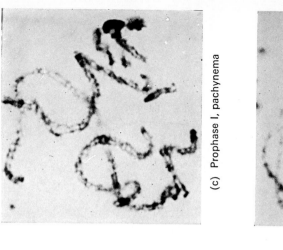

(b) Prophase I, zygonema

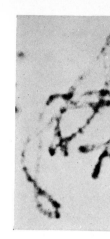

(c) Prophase I, pachynema

(d) Prophase I, early diplonema

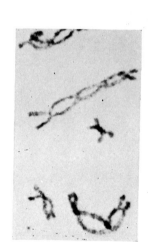

(e) Prophase I, diplonema

(f) Prophase I, mid-diplonema

(g) Prophase I, late diplonema

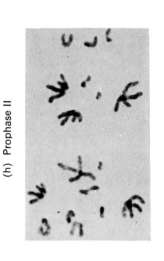

(h) Prophase II

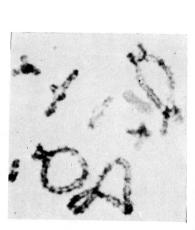

(i) Anaphase II

166. **Meiosis**, stages from orthopteran testis squashes. All Mag. *ca* 975

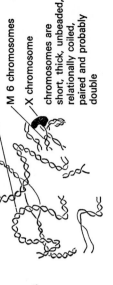

L1⎤
L2⎥ 3 long
L3⎦ chromosomes

M 6 chromosomes

X chromosome

chromosomes are short, thick, unbeaded, relationally coiled, paired and probably double

(c) Prophase I, pachynema

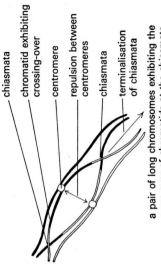

pair of homologous chromosomes

chromosomes are still long, thin, single and beaded but are now in pairs

X chromosome

M 6 chromosomes *condenses near to X chromosome*

(b) Prophase I, zygonema

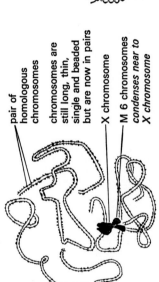

tangled thread of long, thin, single and beaded unpaired chromosomes

chromomeres = *regions of coiling*

pairing just beginning

X chromosome

(a) Prophase I, leptonema

chiasmata

chromatid exhibiting crossing-over

centromere

repulsion between centromeres

chiasmata

terminalisation of chiasmata

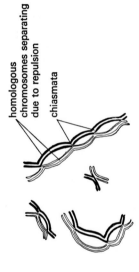

a pair of long chromosomes exhibiting the cross-over of chromatids at the chiasmata

(f) Prophase I, mid-diplonema

homologous chromosomes separating due to repulsion

chiasmata

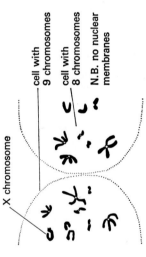

(e) Prophase I, diplonema

chromosome divided into 2 chromatids

relational coiling

homologous pair

a tetrad = *homologous pair of chromosomes, each divided into 2 chromatids*

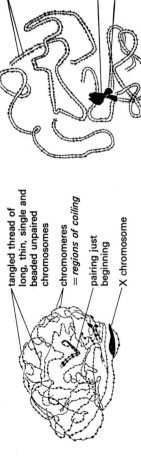

(d) Prophase I, early diplonema

X chromosomes

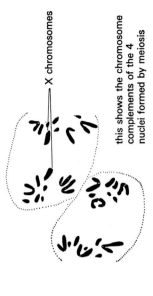

this shows the chromosome complements of the 4 nuclei formed by meiosis

(i) Anaphase II

cell with 9 chromosomes

cell with 8 chromosomes

N.B. no nuclear membranes

X chromosome

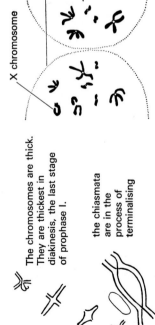

(h) Prophase II

The chromosomes are thick. They are thickest in diakinesis, the last stage of prophase I.

the chiasmata are in the process of terminalising

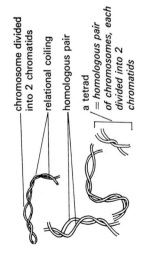

(g) Prophase I, late diplonema

Drawings of Specimens 166a, b, c, d, e, f, g, h, i